The Step-by-Step Guide to Sustainability Planning

The Step-by-Step Guide to Sustainability Planning

How to Create and Implement Sustainability Plans in Any Business or Organization

Darcy Hitchcock and Marsha Willard

with foreword by Alan AtKisson

publishing for a sustainable future

London • Sterling, VA

First published by Earthscan in the UK and USA in 2008

ISBN: 978-1-84407-616-1

Typeset by Domex e-Data Pvt. Ltd, India
Printed and bound in the UK by TJ International, Padstow
Cover design by Yvonne Booth

For a full list of publications please contact:

Earthscan
Dunstan House, 14a St Cross Street
London, EC1N 8XA, UK
Tel: +44 (0)20 7841 1930
Fax: +44 (0)20 7242 1474
Email: earthinfo@earthscan.co.uk
Web: **www.earthscan.co.uk**

22883 Quicksilver Drive, Sterling, VA 20166-2012, USA

Earthscan publishes in association with the International Institute for Environment and Development

A catalogue record for this book is available from the British Library

Library of Congress Cataloging-in-Publication Data

Hitchcock, Darcy E.
  The step-by-step guide to sustainability planning: how to create and implement sustainability plans in any business or organization / Darcy Hitchcock and Marsha Willard ; with foreword by Alan AtKisson.
      p. cm.
  Includes bibliographical references.
  ISBN   978-1-84407-616-1 (pbk.)
  1. Management – Environmental aspects. 2. Sustainable development – Planning
  3. Business planning I. Willard, Marsha L. II. Title.
  HD30.255.H584 2008
  658.4'095–dc22
                                        2008033048

The paper used for this book is FSC certified. FSC (the Forest Stewardship Council) is an international network to promote responsible management of the world's forests.

Mixed Sources
Product group from well-managed
forests and other controlled sources
www.fsc.org Cert no. SGS-COC-2482
© 1996 Forest Stewardship Council

Contents

List of Figures, Tables and Boxes

FIGURES

TABLES

BOXES

Foreword

Alan AtKisson

As a young man, I was literally afraid of cooking. It seemed like complex chemistry to me: one slip with the salt, and the kitchen would probably go up in smoke. Then I came into the possession of an unusually clear little guide called the *Tassajara Cookbook*. It provided almost no actual recipes; instead, it provided the most important general principles, some examples, lists of ingredients, the right sequences for putting ingredients together, and a lot of tips and tricks for making any kind of soup, pie, casserole, stew or whatever else you wanted to create. After reading it, my fear was gone. Suddenly I loved being in the kitchen because I knew something much better than how to follow a recipe: I knew *how to cook*.

The Step-by-Step Guide to Sustainability Planning is very much in the same wonderful tradition of clarity in guidance. If you do not already know how to create and manage a sustainability programme for your company, institution or organization, you soon will. And if you already work with such a programme, these authors have done you the inestimable service of assembling, between two covers, a vast storehouse of how to, when to and where to go for more.

To keep pushing the metaphor, doing sustainability work is very much like making stew. Many ingredients must come together to make a coherent, and tasty, whole. Virtually anything *can* go into it – but not everything *should*. Some things should be done first; other things get thrown in later. And certain things simply do not mix well together at all. There are no short cuts to making stew or to doing sustainability; but there are dead ends, bad choices and blind alleys that can slow you down. This book will help you to avoid these time wasters so that you can get on with the task of achieving results.

There is also no shortage of tools, methods and processes to blend into a basic sustainability programme. These are like spices in a stew, and you will find plenty of room for those here as well. But first one must know, *in general*, how to 'cook up' your organizational sustainability programme in practical terms. And this is the best such cookbook I have seen to date. Twenty years ago, when I was first starting out in professional sustainability work, there was not a cookbook in sight. We made it up as we went along. Today, the number of people working in sustainability (or wanting to) appears to be growing faster than the training programmes, certification standards and other institutional apparatus that normally support a profession. Guides like this book are therefore essential resources, helping to speed people up the learning curve to the point where they, and their organizations, can quickly start contributing to reduced waste, climate neutrality, better performance, increased social justice and the general improvement of well-being for everyone on our increasingly crowded planet. Share this book with as many people as you can.

'But', you might ask, 'you also work as a sustainability consultant, and you have your own book coming out at just the same time, describing your own tools and methods. Why would you write a Foreword endorsing a group of competitors?' First, because this is a very good book. Second, because I believe that all of us working as sustainability practitioners have a number of ethical responsibilities that are special to our profession. One of these involves putting cooperation ahead of competition: when it comes to rescuing the ecological, biological, economic and social systems of our planet from the all-too-real risk of cascading systems failure, we do not have the luxury of competing with each other. Like doctors in the emergency room, with different strengths and specialties, and even personality quirks, we *must* find ways to work together in order to save as many lives as possible. Darcy Hitchcock and Marsha Willard and the Axis Performance team are not my competitors; they are my colleagues and teammates.

In an era of climate change, growing resource scarcity, food riots and more, we are all – together with you, dear reader – struggling to win the biggest competition of all: the ultimate race against time – the transition to a sustainable world.

May 2008
Stockholm, Sweden

Acknowledgements

We wish to thank the following people for reviewing this book and providing anecdotes.

Jeanne Afuvia, Director of Public Policy, Hawaii Institute for Public Affairs
Suhit Anatula, Department of Families and Communities, Government of South Australia
Dorothy Atwood, Zero Waste Alliance
Steve Bicker, NW Natural
Jackie Drumheller, Alaska Airlines
Bill Edmonds, NW Natural
Sara Grigsby, NW Natural
Scott Harris, Simplot
Phil Moran, Stoel Rives
Helen Rigg, Idaho GEM *Stars*
Jill Sughrue, Sustain Northwest
Nancy Stueber, Oregon Museum of Science and Industry
Rick Woodward, Coastwide Laboratories

Thank you, as well, to Rob West at Earthscan for being an advocate for our work and for answering our never-ending questions!

List of Acronyms and Abbreviations

AA	AccountAbility
ANSI	American National Standards Institute
ASTM	American Society for Testing and Materials
BHAG	big, hairy audacious goal
°C	degrees Celsius
CEO	chief executive officer
CERES	Coalition for Environmentally Responsible Economies
CFO	chief financial officer
CO_2	carbon dioxide
CSR	corporate social responsibility
DDT	dichlorodiphenyltrichloroethane
EMS	environmental management system(s)
EPA	US Environmental Protection Agency
EPEAT	Electronic Product Environmental Assessment Tool
EPR	extended producer (or product) responsibility
EuP	energy-using products
°F	degrees Fahrenheit
FSC	Forest Stewardship Council
GHG	greenhouse gas
GRI	Global Reporting Initiative
ha	hectare
ISO	International Organization for Standardization
JTS	journey to sustainability
kWh	kilowatt hours
lb	pound
LED	light-emitting diode
LEED	Leadership in Energy and Environmental Design (green building tool)
LEED-EB	LEED for existing buildings
MBDC	McDonough Braungart Design Chemistry
MDG	United Nations Millennium Development Goal

NGO	non-governmental organization
OMSI	Oregon Museum of Science and Industry
PBDE	polybrominated diphenyl ether
PCB	polychlorinated biphenyl
PDF	portable document format
PLA	polylactic acid
3 Rs	reduce, reuse and recycle
REACH	Registration, Evaluation, Authorization and Restriction of Chemicals
RFP	request for proposal
RoHS	European Union Restriction of Hazardous Substances Directive
SA	Social Accountability
SC	system condition from The Natural Step framework
SCORE	Sustainability Competency and Opportunity Rating and Evaluation
SFI	Sustainable Forestry Initiative
SMS	sustainability management system
SOP	standard operating procedure
SWOT	strengths, weaknesses, opportunities and threats
TNS	The Natural Step
UK	United Kingdom
US	United States
VOC	volatile organic compound
WBCSD	World Business Council on Sustainable Development
WCED	World Commission on Environment and Development
WEEE	Waste Electrical and Electronic Equipment Directive

Introduction

Sustainability is a hot business trend and many organizations are pursuing it, some with greater success than others. Years ago, you could just muddle along making random green efforts to earn a gold star in the marketplace. Now, however, as stakeholders have become more sophisticated, it's important to undertake a formal process for approaching sustainability. Sustainability planning involves setting a strategy, figuring out what you need to work on, and orchestrating a series of projects over the long term to reach sustainability. A couple of years ago, one of our clients asked: 'What should go into a sustainability plan? Isn't there an accepted format?' At the time, we had no good answer; there was no accepted standard or template for creating these plans. While the Global Reporting Initiative is intended to provide standardization for reporting, it exceeds what many organizations can or need to report. It also may not represent all you will want to track internally. The lack of a template has wasted resources. Everyone was reinventing the process. We decided to systematize it.

After working with a wide variety of organizations to develop these plans and reports, we have refined the process down to a systematic and easily replicated set of steps. Of course, this is not the only way to create a sustainability plan and report. But our process will provide you with a template for how to do your own. This book is a cookbook of sorts, providing you with a well-tested recipe for creating your own sustainability plan and report. You can substitute ingredients and customize the steps as you see fit. Like most cooks, you may prefer to follow the recipe closely the first time around; but as your familiarity grows, you can increasingly modify the recipe to suit your tastes.

It is now becoming standard practice for organizations to create a sustainability plan and report. Approximately 75 per cent of the largest corporations now produce a sustainability report or corporate social responsibility report and this trend has been accelerating. Increasingly, investors and other stakeholders expect to have access to this information. The Carbon Disclosure Project, for example, has put pressure on companies to report their climate-related risks. Others produce these reports to enhance their image. This practice is being pushed down into the supply chain as well. Similarly, many governmental agencies and departments are also being asked to create a sustainability plan and report on their progress.

Of course, some organizations still fly by the seat of their pants without a flight plan. For some period of time, they simply pursue the most obvious projects. There are risks in this approach, though. How do you know you're working on the most important impacts? Are you confident that the changes you implement now won't be dead ends? Are there blind spots in your approach that will come back to bite you later? How do you ensure that you are addressing the full definition of sustainability as opposed to window dressing in a few areas? Do you have the systems in place to support your effort so that it won't fizzle out? The only way to get a good handle on what you should be working on is to do the analysis associated with a sustainability plan.

In the broadest sense, sustainability planning revolves around two main questions: should we pursue sustainability and if so, how? You may think your organization has already committed to sustainability; but understanding the business case evolves over time. Certainly, if this is your organization's first time in creating a sustainability plan, you should spend time on the first question. In future years, you may be able to gloss over it, just checking to see if your sustainability policy still captures your intent.

This book will help you to answer these questions in a systematic way. We have created a set of electronic files to support this process called SPaRK™, the Sustainability Planning and

Table I.1 *Questions you will want to answer*

Should we pursue (or continue to pursue) sustainability?	If yes, what will we do?
What is it about sustainability that makes sense for us? What pressures are pushing us to do it? What opportunities does it present? Are there certain issues within sustainability that are a particular focus (e.g. climate change, e-waste and international labour standards)?	What would a fully sustainable vision for our organization look like?
	What frameworks will we use to define sustainability in our context?
How does sustainability relate to other organizational initiatives (e.g. lean manufacturing, environmental management systems and product certification)?	How will we measure our progress?
	What projects will we undertake, now and in the future to reach a sustainable state?
Where should we start or implement sustainability next?	What systems and structures will we need to support our efforts?
What are the likely challenges and how can we overcome them?	
What else do we need to know to make a decision?	
Is this the right time?	

Reporting Kit. It includes an Excel file with spreadsheets for the most common analyses and metrics. This file is linked to an MS Word template for an internal sustainability plan and report such that the charts and graphs are automatically pulled into it. Please see our website for more information about this tool (www.axisperformance.com).

WHO SHOULD READ THIS BOOK?

This book will be most helpful for people who must plan and lead an effort to create a sustainability plan and report. Individuals may include:

- city managers, council members and corporate executives who want to direct their staff to create a sustainability plan and/or report;
- sustainability directors and coordinators;
- consultants who want to make sustainability planning part of their services;
- academics who want to teach their students how to develop a sustainability plan.

HOW THIS BOOK IS STRUCTURED

Following a general chapter on organizational change principles (see Chapter 1), the chapters in this book each represent a major step in the process of creating a sustainability plan and report. Each chapter has two sections: background reading to prepare you to do the step and then a set of exercises you can use to perform the task. The chapters are laid out roughly in chronological or linear order; but as you can see in Figure I.1, some of the steps can be done in a different order. The real world isn't linear; so use your judgement about where to start and the order in which you want to do the steps.

BOX I.1 TIP: KEEP MOMENTUM WITH QUICK WINS

People differ in their abilities and comfort with abstract cognitive tasks such as planning. When we have clients with a preference for action, we may allocate a portion of the planning meetings to identifying and acting on low-hanging fruit. One client identified a few small projects that were no-brainers – reducing lighting levels by removing bulbs from fixtures and improving their recycling system – which we addressed in parallel with the planning process. This helped the participants to feel a sense of accomplishment and tangible results while we worked on the longer-range plan.

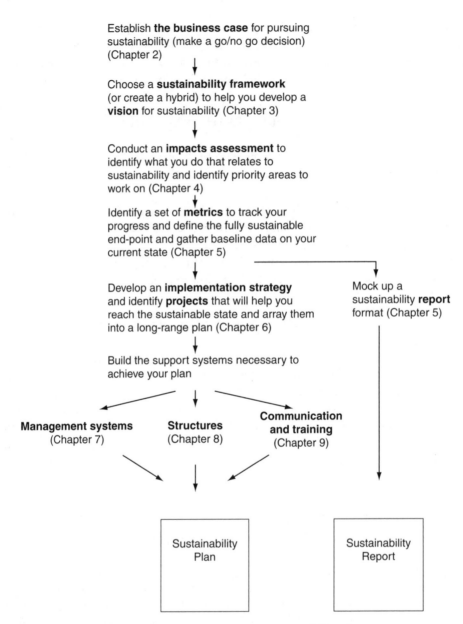

Figure I.1 *Steps to creating a sustainability plan*

DEFINITION OF TERMS USED IN THIS BOOK AND PROCESS

This section lists the terms that we use in this book as we describe the process for creating a sustainability plan:

- *Vision*: what sustainability means in your situation – in other words, your applied definition of sustainability. Your vision is what a fully sustainable version of your organization might be like.
- *Framework*: a generally recognized way of knowing what sustainability means. The two most common examples are the triple bottom line and The Natural Step. Ideally, a framework will define the full set of issues that should be addressed and make it clear what a fully sustainable state would look like. The framework should inform your vision.
- *Metrics*: how you express your intent or vision in measurable terms; a measure of how sustainable you are (e.g. greenhouse gases and energy use per product).
- *Sustainable end point*: the target for the metrics; what you are shooting for when you are fully sustainable (e.g. 100 per cent climate neutral; 15kWh per product). Note that some of these end points will be driven by science and/or The Natural Step framework, while others will be a judgement call based on your knowledge of your operation and the industry.
- *Sustainable criteria*: provides further definition of what qualifies as 'sustainable' or not (e.g. criteria for defining sustainable agricultural products might include local, certified and/or organic). Defines what you would accept as counting towards the goal.
- *Goals*: intermediate steps to get to the sustainable end point. (e.g. reduce greenhouse gases by 10 per cent in 2009, 25 per cent in 2012, etc.).

SUSTAINABILITY PLANS VERSUS ASSESSMENTS – WHAT'S THE DIFFERENCE AND WHICH DO YOU NEED?

Our clients often confuse sustainability planning and sustainability assessments, asking for one when they need the other. And sometimes they need both. Let us compare and contrast them below.

Sustainability assessments

Think of a sustainability assessment as your annual physical. Your doctor palpitates and listens and then gives you an assessment of how healthy you are. He or she may also identify some things you need to work on, such as lowering your blood pressure. This may lead to more detailed assessments (e.g. a cholesterol test). A handful of actions are identified, including entreaties to eat better and to try a new prescription. However, these recommendations are not, in themselves, likely to be all you need to address in order to live a good life.

Similarly, sustainability assessments such as our SCORE™ assessment give you a snapshot of how healthy your sustainability effort is and what you need to work on. While these assessments typically prescribe some next steps, they do not (nor does your annual physical) give you a detailed long-term plan for improving the state of affairs. Assessments often lead to more questions, which imply additional assessments. SCORE™, for example, measures the degree to which you have embedded sustainability within your business practices. Other types of assessments are often helpful. You may want to assess your strategic position in the marketplace, or evaluate levels of greenhouse gas emissions, energy consumed or waste.

The assessments you choose determine the information you get; so select assessments wisely. Your blood pressure might be high because your marriage is in ruins; but the cholesterol test won't show that, and many doctors won't think to ask; they just whip out their prescription pad.

In the context of sustainability, it's important to do an overarching impact analysis so that you know what you are responsible for and what your priorities are. Do they include solid waste? Energy? Paper? International labour practices? Then you can conduct detailed assessments of these priority areas. Otherwise, you may risk wasting money gathering data on unimportant areas, and the data will become stale long before you need them.

Assessments are useful after you have completed some initial steps, including clarifying the business case and undertaking initial projects. We had a client who asked to do SCORE™ before they'd even made an organizational commitment to sustainability. We said that was like assessing your ability to play the violin before determining that you wanted to play one. It's cruel to all involved to hold a recital before you have practised!

Sustainability assessments, then, are useful when you:

- have decided to pursue sustainability;
- have undertaken at least some preliminary sustainability-related actions;
- need baseline data for those areas you have targeted for improvement;
- want a formal assessment of how you are doing and how far you have come;
- aren't sure what to work on next.

Sustainability planning

If sustainability assessments are like your annual physical, then sustainability planning is analogous to life planning. It determines what's important to you and builds a long-term plan to get there. A life plan asks you to assess not only your physical health, but also the state of your relationships, finances, work life and spiritual development. You are prompted to define your mission in life, and you set goals and develop plans in all of these areas.

Similarly, sustainability planning, at least as we conceptualize it, involves clarifying the business case for pursuing sustainability and defining a vision for a fully sustainable version of your organization. It includes developing metrics for tracking your progress and a long-term plan to achieve your goals.

Sustainability planning is useful when you:

- have a clear organizational intention to pursue sustainability and want a systematic way to approach its implementation;
- need to make overarching decisions that will help you to manage the sustainability effort (e.g. define common metrics and frameworks that all parts of the organization will use);
- need a shared understanding of what you are trying to achieve and why;
- lack a long-term plan for achieving your sustainability vision and goals.

Sustainability planning is usually an iterative process where you revisit your goals and priorities, check on progress and revise the plan year after year. Sustainability assessments, on the other hand, tend to be episodic, occurring when you have reached a plateau or when you want a quantifiable progress check.

When you need both

Sustainability assessments can be part of a larger sustainability planning process. Some sustainability assessments, including an impact assessment, are core to our planning process. We explain a few such assessments in this book. However, we do not cover sustainability assessments in exhaustive detail here.

Other assessments, such as our SCORE™ assessment, can be integrated within a sustainability process. They typically fit into the process in one of three places:

1   *At the beginning.* Clients who have already undertaken some sustainability-related initiatives may want to begin with an assessment that reveals their strengths and areas for improvement. These insights can then catalyse a sustainability planning process if they don't already have one, or the insights can be integrated within an existing sustainability plan.
2   *Before the impact assessment.* A high-level assessment such as SCORE™ can help you to identify the parts of the impact assessment to focus on. For example, if purchasing

comes up as a weak area, you can then get into more detail when you complete the materials portion of the impact assessment.

3   *During the data-gathering phase.* Clients may want to include other sustainability assessments as data points. They can introduce other perspectives that should be incorporated within the planning process. SCORE™, for example, is a powerful educational tool, helping managers to understand what sustainability means in their context; and it provides quantifiable data that can be used as a baseline against which they compare progress year after year. You may also want to conduct other such assessments, including a systems audit, greenhouse gas inventory, social audit or waste assessment.

RESOURCES

Broad sustainability assessment tools

These assessment tools may be helpful to use as part of your planning process:

- SCORE™ measures how well you have integrated sustainability within your business practices (see www.axisperformance.com).
- STARS is a similar assessment for higher education, created by the Association for the Advancement of Sustainability in Higher Education (see www.aashe.org).
- S-BAR is still under development at the time of writing, but should provide useful data, comparable across businesses within a sector (see www.sustainabilityratings.com).

TAILORING A PLANNING PROCESS TO YOUR NEEDS

Plan to deepen your sophistication over time. For organizations which are starting on the road to sustainability, our bias is to get through the planning process quickly so they can get onto tangible projects that demonstrate results. Think of this as a learning spiral. Each year, you will need to produce a sustainability plan; but as you become more sophisticated, so will your plan. As you read this book, do not assume that you have to do all the exercises in each chapter before moving on. Choose the ones that make sense for you now. Do a reasonable job of performing each step. Next year, add elements that push you to a deeper level. We provide a few sample approaches in the following sections to show you how to cluster these tasks into meetings.

BOX I.2 EARTHSCAN'S SUSTAINABILITY PLAN AND REPORT: THREE YEARS IN THE MAKING

Earthscan, our publisher, has a staff of under 20 people, but manages a worldwide supply chain of editors, proofreaders, typesetters, printers, distributors and marketing staff. Like most small businesses, they are swamped doing their day-to-day work; so it has taken special effort to build a sustainability plan and report. It's taken them about three years to refine their approach so that it adequately reflects their impacts and strategies, resulting in a sustainability report that they feel good about sharing with the public. Getting climate-related data was particularly challenging, stretching out the data-gathering process. They felt that it was important to take responsibility for the greenhouse gases associated with paper production since these emissions dwarfed those associated with their own operations, including the transportation of books around the world.

Fast track to a sustainability plan

If this is the first time your organization has written a sustainability plan, then the following approach is probably the level of detail that is appropriate unless you have a very large and complex operation. You don't want to overwhelm people with analysis or concepts. We often do this process in five to six half-day meetings or two to three whole-day meetings. It is usually done either with top management or a sustainability steering committee.

Note that some of the steps don't follow the order of our chapters. While this book is laid out in a logical and linear fashion, we often shuffle the order of the later steps. The early steps should be done in sequence. You have to know what sustainability is before you can determine why you want to pursue it; and you have to know what your impacts are before you can establish goals and metrics. After that, it almost doesn't matter what the order is in which you perform the steps. Be flexible and adopt an order that makes sense to you for a particular situation.

Between meetings, communicate the results of each meeting; conduct the impacts assessment at a departmental level, if desired. Solicit feedback from key stakeholders on the business case and framework.

Between meetings, complete a metrics worksheet for any metrics that you do not currently track. Gather baseline data on your major metrics. Communicate with appropriate stakeholders about the results of the meeting and solicit project ideas.

Table I.2 *Sample fast-track agenda: Day 1*

Topic	Content	Chapter reference	Estimated time
Sustainability frameworks and concepts	Provide a briefing on sustainability: review common sustainability frameworks and determine which one (or a hybrid) is going to best serve you. Cover only those frameworks that are most likely to be relevant (e.g. triple bottom line, The Natural Step or the Global Reporting Initiative).	See the background reading and framework-based visioning in Chapter 3.	One to three hours
Business case	Refine the business case: by examining both threats and opportunities, refine your intentions and hopes for sustainability. It's important to tie sustainability to your overall strategy. This can help to guide your priorities.	You may choose to use either the worldwide trends cards or threats and opportunities exercises from Chapter 2.	One to two hours
Impact assessment	Conduct a high-level impact assessment for the organization as a whole and choose priority areas. This same process can be done again at the department and work-group level if desired now or in future years.	Use the high-level impact assessment from Chapter 4. If desired, use the opportunity finder from Chapter 6.	One hour

After the meeting, refine the information developed in the meetings into a sustainability plan document. Conduct a team pre-launch from Chapter 8 for any near-term projects.

This approach is best done with time between the sessions (not a three-day marathon) in order to allow time for ideas to percolate, to solicit reactions from key stakeholders and to gather data that isn't at your fingertips.

Table I.3 *Sample fast-track agenda: Day 2*

Topic	Content	Chapter reference	Estimated time
Structures	Determine the structure for your sustainability efforts.	Use the sustainability structure exercise from Chapter 8 and refer to the incubator level for the plan implement–monitor–review charts and the sustainability management system (SMS) process summary in Chapter 7.	One hour
Project criteria	Determine the criteria you want to use to choose projects. Do you want the whole organization working on the same effort? Do you want individual departments each to come up with one additional goal?	In Chapter 6, discuss the issues in the section on 'Managing the load' and create a table similar to Tables 6.2 and 6.3. Or use the exercise in the section on 'Developing a system for choosing projects'.	One hour
Metrics	Develop a set of sustainability metrics. Focus on major impacts and likely project areas (you may be able to combine the vision discussion with the creation of metrics).	Use the suggested metrics for the framework you've chosen from Chapter 5 and/or create a sustainability scorecard, as outlined in the chapter.	One to two hours
Report format	Mock up the structure of your year-end sustainability report.	Use the sustainability report template from Chapter 5.	One to two hours

Variations on the process for more advanced organizations

In future years, you can beef up your process in the following ways:

- *Policy*: once you have some working knowledge of sustainability in your organization, you can develop a formal policy statement for the board of directors or city council to approve (see the section on 'Sustainability policy' in Chapter 7). Many organizations like to do this as part of their first sustainability plan since it sets the plan in context. However, sometimes it's instructive to get some experience behind you before top

Table I.4 *Sample fast-track agenda: Day 3*

Topic	Content	Chapter reference	Estimated time
Plan	Develop a two- to three-year plan, identifying major organization-wide initiatives.	See the section on 'Developing a long-term plan to reach sustainability' in Chapter 6.	Two to four hours
Systems	Determine a method for coordinating and tracking efforts of individual departments, if needed.	Use the SMS process summary or gap analysis from Chapter 7.	Two hours
Communication and training	Develop a basic communication and training plan to support your sustainability plan.	See the communication plan in Chapter 9.	Two hours

management is ready to put a formal commitment into writing. One client waited seven years before getting around to this, preferring instead to focus on tangible action. Organizations that attempt to write a policy too soon often have to rewrite it a year or two later. Ideally, you want a policy statement to have more longevity; so write it when the executives and board are well enough steeped in sustainability to create an informed and inspired policy.

- *Sustainability assessment*: it can be helpful to do a formal assessment of your performance. See the earlier section on 'Resources: Broad sustainability assessment tools' in this chapter for some suggestions.
- *Vision*: at some point, your organization will be psychologically ready to challenge its own business model. Eventually, everyone realizes that 'they can't get there from here' and that there are elements of their business model that are fundamentally unsustainable. Exercises that can help you to examine these issues include 'Backcasting' from Chapter 3 or the 'Long-term sustainability strategy' from Chapter 2.
- *Impacts*: as you learn more about sustainability, you may discover impacts that you were blind to at first. Doing the impact assessment at a more detailed level, sometimes for a specific work process, can be helpful. See the other alternatives in Chapter 4.
- *Metrics*: many organizations start out with an incomplete set of metrics, or at least incomplete data on all their metrics. Over time, you should develop a complete and balanced set with baseline data and performance trends. See Chapter 5 on metrics.

- *Management systems*: over time, you are likely to need to strengthen your sustainability management system, both because you are more sophisticated and have more going on, but also because the demands of the world continue to ratchet up. See Chapter 7 on management systems.
- *Training*: as your sustainability efforts progress, you will have two main training challenges. The first is to ensure that as you have turnover: that new people are properly trained on your frameworks and methods. Second, your need for knowledge will gradually deepen. The field is progressing rapidly; new methods are being developed all the time; employees will be ready to learn more advanced skills. A training plan will become increasingly important (see Chapter 9).

  Work is under way through the International Society of Sustainability Professionals to develop a list of competencies that those working in the sustainability field should have. As consensus forms around these competencies and as certifications and accreditations become available, use these to inform your understanding of the skills your employees need to develop.
- *Communication*: as your efforts progress, you will also likely communicate with more and more stakeholders. At first, you may keep all of the communication in-house. But increasingly you'll need to communicate with other stakeholders, including customers, suppliers, non-governmental organizations (NGOs), trade associations and the like. Invest more time in planning for these relationships (see Chapter 9).
- *Reporting*: over time, your sustainability report will become increasingly detailed and sophisticated. Assess your report against the Global Reporting Initiative guidelines (see Chapter 8).

1
Preparing for Change

Before you embark on your sustainability planning process, we want to present you with some general concepts about change and the principles or conditions that contribute to successful implementation of new programmes in organizations. Introducing a change of any kind to an organization can be a delicate proposition. We have seen (and likely you have experienced) many failed initiatives. Our intent in this chapter is to arm you with information and strategies on organizational change so that your sustainability initiative will be largely protected from the common pitfalls of many change efforts.

Implementing a sustainability programme is, in many ways, the same as implementing any other change initiative. Perhaps your organization has been successful with past initiatives: re-engineering, total quality management, lean manufacturing, self-directed work teams or any other of the popular 20th-century management improvement strategies. There are valuable lessons to be learned (from both the successes and failures) that can be carried over and applied to your sustainability programme. Consider the general principles below that we have gleaned from over two decades of consulting with organizations.

Keys to success in any organizational change initiative

Every new initiative needs to be grounded in a solid business rationale. If it doesn't make business sense to do – that is, if it doesn't return some value to the organization – it will be difficult for people to make it a priority and likely to fall to the bottom of the list of things to do. Chapter 2 will help you to craft the business case in order to help ensure that it becomes and stays a priority for your organization. In addition, consider the following aspects as well.

Create a sense of urgency. There's nothing like a 'burning platform' to incite enthusiasm, and it's getting easier and easier to find one. A burning platform creates motivation to move forward because, in part, it makes it clear that the status quo is no longer viable. Does the recent spike in energy costs affect your business? Are your customers suspicious of your operations? What about the Kyoto Accord and climate change? One organization used pictures of its employees' children as the backdrop to its sustainability kick-off meeting to emphasize the impact that it will have on future generations.

Find a champion and get leadership support. Ideally, you should find someone with some position of authority to champion your effort and to ensure that it gets the time, attention and resources it will require for a meaningful impact. The higher up in your organization your champion is, the greater the likelihood that your effort will have staying power. These people often go by the title of sustainability director or coordinator. In addition, you will eventually need top management support. We have never seen a change effort succeed and stick without leadership support. That doesn't mean your effort has to start with leadership; but top management support *and* involvement are key to long-term success. This means that leaders need to not only talk about sustainability, but also back their words up with symbolic and substantive action.

Find a logical starting point. Sometimes the place to begin is obvious. If you are constructing a new building, adding a new production line or making other decisions with long-term ramifications, then start there. Often, though, you will have to consider the general scope of your effort; whether to start in a portion of the organization or implement it across the whole business. Is there a department that is eager and ripe for this? Is there a problem you are trying to solve or risk you are trying to avoid? Do you need a safe place to experiment, far from the glaring lights of the media or your customers? Are there certain departments or people who are raring to go? Think strategically about how broad your effort should be. Is it better to begin small and nurture the initiative or to broadcast your intentions organization wide and roll the whole effort out with a bang?

Sometimes, it's best to start quietly, letting the effort evolve over time, starting by tucking sustainability into logical places, not making a big deal about it. This approach is appropriate when you don't have a huge looming problem driving you to pursue sustainability and/or you don't have top management support. This can also be a good approach if employees are jaded by past change initiatives and when your business case for pursuing sustainability is still developing.

In other situations, it's best to broadcast that you are doing something new and make a big splash. In this situation, sustainability is discussed explicitly as an objective; audacious goals are set; everyone is expected to rethink what they do through the lens of sustainability. This approach is appropriate when top management has made an enduring commitment to sustainability and when it is important to signal a significant change of corporate strategy (e.g. to disgruntled customers, shareholders or the public.) This can also be an appropriate approach if you are trying to use sustainability to create a new, more empowered and committed corporate culture.

Attach your project to existing efforts. To avoid the 'programme of the month' cynicism, it can be helpful to explicitly link your sustainability efforts to familiar programmes in the organization. It's often easier to add another consideration to an existing project than to generate the interest and energy in starting something entirely new. You may already, for example, have lean manufacturing or quality teams. If so, ask them to include broader sustainability-related issues in the work that they do. If your organization already thinks in terms of corporate social responsibility, then just refine the definition to include criteria related to the limits of nature. Do you have an environmental management system that could be strengthened to be a sustainability management system? Is your organization a long-time advocate of total quality management, lean manufacturing or related efforts? Do you have a longstanding practice of empowering employee work teams? If so, perhaps you can show how sustainability is a logical extension of them.

In Table 1.1, we list common existing organizational change initiatives and describe how sustainability can be dovetailed with them.

Communicate constantly. Once you are ready to 'go public' with your efforts, you will need to be diligent about keeping people informed of what's going on. Sustainability will likely be a new concept for many in your organization, so in addition to the constant stream of communication about your progress, you may also need to continuously educate people about sustainability and why it is important. We've learned that your communication efforts should involve multiple media (email, presentations, discussion groups, etc.) and include opportunities for two-way communication in conversations and meetings.

Share your results. While many of your projects may leave people feeling good about what you have done, they will have much more value if you have hard data to support your claims of success. Tracking the impact will not only maintain enthusiasm, but will bolster your ability to sell additional projects down the line.

Create opportunities for involvement. Eventually you will also need fairly wide involvement across the organization. This usually implies forming teams or committees to contribute to both the planning and execution of your ideas. We've also learned that you don't need

---

BOX 1.1 CASCADE CORPORATION: MAKING SENSE OF ALL THEIR EFFORTS

Cascade Corporation, an international manufacturer of forklifts, was a long-time advocate of empowerment and self-directed work teams. It deployed lean manufacturing principles to improve its efficiencies and to eliminate waste, and was already ISO 9000 certified and working on ISO 14001 at most sites. Its board cautioned the corporation to begin thinking more about social responsibility since its programmes appeared to be disconnected and disjointed. We showed Cascade how sustainability could be an umbrella to connect all of its efforts, while at the same time identifying additional blind spots that it should consider addressing.

Table 1.1 *Points of entry*

Supply chain/purchasing	One way of becoming more sustainable is to begin choosing greener products, supporting greener vendors and reducing what you buy. *Example projects*: product substitution, purchasing audits and green building.
Environmental management system (EMS)	If you have an EMS, you can embed sustainability criteria within your selection process for setting objectives and choosing projects. *Example projects*: expand eco-metrics to become a full set of sustainability metrics; develop a method for evaluating potential projects using a sustainability framework as a filter.
Lean manufacturing/total quality management	Sustainability is a logical fit with waste reduction and efficiency efforts. *Example projects*: zero waste, resource maximization, de-materialization and product redesign.
Teams	If you have a history of using teams (e.g. project teams or safety teams), you can assign sustainability-related projects to one or more teams. *Example projects*: finding more benign chemicals; reducing waste going to the landfill; improving resource efficiency.
Strategic planning	One way of exposing executives to sustainability is to include it as one of many trends that they should examine during their strategic 'environmental scan'. *Example projects*: site visits to sustainable competitors or customers, benchmarking and backcasting.
Corporate social responsibility (CSR)	CSR is sometimes used as a synonym for sustainability; but often it omits important components. Is your CSR effort focused on social impacts without taking account of nature's limits? Is it focused on protecting your image, but misses out on strategic opportunities? You can enlarge your definition of CSR to include all the elements of sustainability. *Example projects*: introduce a science-based framework such as The Natural Step. Assess your CSR report against the Global Reporting Initiative (GRI) and see where your holes are.

absolutely everybody on board. Critical mass seems to be around 15 to 20 per cent of the members of the organization. If you have the active involvement of at least that many people, you will likely affect an organization-wide change.

> ## BOX 1.2 OREGON MUSEUM OF SCIENCE AND INDUSTRY: GETTING BUY-IN FROM EMPLOYEES
>
> When Nancy Stueber was promoted to president of the Oregon Museum of Science and Industry (OMSI), she already knew she wanted to integrate sustainability within their operations. But her organization did not respond well to top-down edicts. Nancy needed to know if the employees would support this. So we helped her to form a diagonal-slice steering committee whose job was to study sustainability for a year, implement a couple of pilot efforts and then recommend a go–no-go decision. The steering committee, after analysing its opportunities, decided to focus on climate and waste. Since there was already an energy audit being conducted – which would have the largest impact on their greenhouse gases – they chose to focus on alternative commuting, in part because it would give employees a tangible way of participating in the efforts. This also helped them to address a local regulatory requirement for trip reductions. The zero-waste task force conducted a waste audit and provided data for each department and the organization over all. During the year, Nancy and the steering committee did a number of things to educate employees about sustainability and the organization's efforts. After a year, the steering committee gave sustainability a thumb's up. It is now one of OMSI's strategic values, integral to its strategic planning efforts.

Manage personal transitions. Since the changes implied by a move towards sustainability have broad impact across the organization, you will need to be prepared to handle the impact of that on employees and to manage the personal transitions of the people affected. Transition management theory posits that people go through three predictable stages: a stage of loss for the old way of doing things (even when the old way was problematic or undesirable); a period of adjustment where they start to see the possibilities in the new methods; and, finally, a stage of acceptance and integration. Develop strategies that are appropriate to these stages to ensure that people manage the transition smoothly.

Manage external stakeholders. In addition to employee management, your initiative needs to take into account how the change will be experienced by your external stakeholders. Don't forget to address the impact that might be felt by your vendors, your stockholders or your community. Each of these players has the ability to derail your efforts if sufficiently upset, as well as to contribute to its progress if they are involved and kept appraised.

Work towards system integration. Lastly, remember that like any significant change, the principles and strategies related to your sustainability effort will eventually need to be integrated within the fabric of the organization. In the end, it may require adjusting or adapting your core business systems, like those that control hiring, compensation, purchasing, contracts, accounting processes and the like.

Special considerations for sustainability initiatives

While sustainability initiatives share many of the same requirements for success as other change efforts, the topic of sustainability also brings its own special issues. Consider the following list of considerations and strategies for addressing them.

Make sustainability understandable. First of all, sustainability can be an abstract concept that many people have difficulty understanding. It often results in a paradigm shift for people, creating a whole new way of looking at the world. Your training and communication efforts should take this into account by translating sustainability into meaningful language, providing examples and demonstrating direct applications.

Manage both short and long term. The scale and timeframes associated with sustainability are also hard to grasp. The predicted 2° to 6° rise in global temperatures, for example, doesn't sound like much to people who don't understand the implications. In addition, the real impact of that change may not be felt for many years, perhaps long after some of us are gone. Typically, organizational change initiatives take two to five years to realize. With sustainability we talk in 10- to 20-year horizons. How many of your employees expect to be with your organization in 20 years? This highlights the importance of including quick wins in your sustainability plan to keep the effort alive and real to the people who will be implementing it.

Stay above the details. Sustainability often also involves scientific or technical language and concepts. You can expect eyes to start glazing over when the conversation gets too technical. Some of the science that relates to sustainability issues is also still uncertain or not completely precise. This may contribute to debate within your organization about the need to address sustainability as well as the strategies for ensuring it. Keeping the focus on the broad concept and vision highlighting that sustainability is about health (economic, social and environmental) will help. In addition, remind people that not all problems can be solved with today's thinking or technology and that the near future could open up new approaches and information.

Manage the emotional impact. Sustainability can also be an emotionally charged topic. It's easy to tap into the guilt people carry about our lifestyles and their impacts on the planet. For people with children, this can be especially so as they can have a strong visceral response to problems that future generations will inherit. There is also the baggage connected with the historical environmental movement: being an environmentalist often meant being anti-business or a granola-eating, tree-hugging radical. Chapter 2, which deals with the business case, will arm you to address this latter challenge. Dealing with the emotional issues is tougher. We've learned, though, that there is magic in empowering people to do something positive and to be sure that each person has the opportunity to contribute.

Decide what you are going to call the effort. In some situations, more during the past than now, the term 'sustainability' was a liability. If your organization has a long history of total quality management, you may choose to frame sustainability as 'enlarging the definition of quality to include society and nature'. In manufacturing, 'zero waste' might be a strong catch phrase to describe the intent. In healthcare, phrasing that refers to 'patient, community and environmental health' might make sense to people. Architects might get excited about 'living buildings' and 'smart growth', and governmental planners might like 'livability'. If the term sustainability is going to be more of a barrier than an asset, translate the concept into terms that will be more meaningful.

What to do before creating a sustainability plan

A lot of groundwork has been laid before an organization is ready to work on a sustainability plan. You need to have a clear business case in order to pursue it, as well as sufficient support. If your organization isn't quite ready to create a sustainability plan, the following tasks may be useful.

Determine your current stage of development. Perhaps the best place to start your own sustainability initiative is by assessing your current relationship with the issue. We've identified several phases or steps that organizations tend to go through on their path towards higher sophistication and understanding (see Figure 1.1).

On the low end are organizations that are still only focused on regulatory compliance. Organizations at this level are primarily concerned with avoiding legal liabilities and may view environmental issues as a source of additional costs and headaches. Organizations focusing on eco-efficiencies have discovered that saving resources not only helps the environment, but also their financial bottom line. The focus of these two perspectives is internal. At some point, many organizations realize that being 'green' can attract new customers or make their community more attractive. They use green marketing to differentiate themselves from their competitors.

Both green marketing and eco-efficiencies focus on 'doing better'. However, when organizations understand sustainability, they begin to wonder: 'Are we doing enough?'

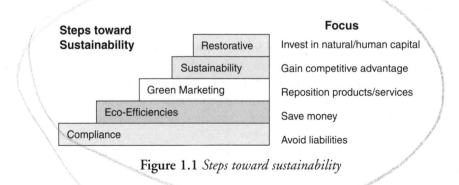

Figure 1.1 *Steps toward sustainability*

When organizations reach the level of sustainability, they understand in their hearts the need to significantly change what they're doing and also understand in their heads the incredible business opportunity that this can afford. Some businesses are starting to talk about going beyond sustainability (which balances our demands with what nature can provide) to restoration, rebuilding what we have degraded.

If your organization is focused on compliance, you may be able to convince people that achieving more than just compliance can save money (eco-efficiencies). If your organization understands eco-efficiencies, can you think of ways that you could leverage that better-than-compliance stance to impress others outside of your organization (green marketing)? If your organization understands the advantages of being 'green', maybe you can convince people of the competitive opportunities in becoming sustainable in order to push the envelope on what it means to be 'green'. Don't try to jump too many steps at one time.

Plant the seed. Something has to nudge (or shove) an organization out of the status quo. Sometimes organizations are confronted with an immediate environmental or social issue and have to make a quick adjustment: a major customer refuses to buy a product because of toxic chemicals; a company is losing market share and needs a way to differentiate itself; new environmental regulations increase the costs associated with a major raw material; new scientific findings bring significant public pressure for change.

If you are in a situation where your organization has a significant problem related to sustainability, you should find it relatively easy to get support for your efforts. It should be clear to all that change is necessary. Begin by selling the problem. Make sure everyone knows what the problem is and how it links to sustainability. The drawback to this situation is that you must often react quickly, under enormous pressure, which is usually more costly than if your organization had foreseen this problem. You may want to put together a swat team to work on designing solutions to the immediate problem; but also begin educating everyone about the need to pursue sustainability so that once the immediate problem is solved, you don't become complacent and caught by surprise again.

If you don't have a pressing problem, then maybe you can tap into personal passion. In this situation, it's important to understand who has that passion. Does the chief executive officer (CEO) or executive director have the passion or does it originate from somewhere in the middle of the organization? When top management grabs onto sustainability, they can use normal formal business channels to implement it. Their first challenge will be to inspire others to share their passion. Leaders need to offer both rational and emotional reasons for getting involved. This is the time for the 'I have a dream' speeches that, like Martin Luther King's famous oratory, paint a clear and compelling vision of a better future.

On the other hand, if the person with passion is somewhere in the bowels of the organization, he or she will not be able to use these formal channels. In this situation, you need an incubator: a protected, quiet place in the organization where you can nurture the development of a couple of high-potential projects. Gather pre- and post-data so that you can show a positive financial return. Then, when your 'baby' is adequately established, start publicizing your results.

Table 1.2 summarizes how you might approach sustainability with and without top management support.

Gather like-minded people. Many sustainability efforts begin with a small, lonely band of people who begin meeting to discuss what they wish could happen. Reach out to others. Speak from the heart. Discover who else shares your passion. You might be surprised. Begin meeting and finding things you can do that will educate yourselves and others. Gather data to build the business case and take on low-cost, low-risk projects that others will appreciate.

Ideally, you can formally convene people for these early conversations. We are not fans of the voluntary 'green teams' that meet over lunch without any formal authority or clear link to the business because they send the message that this is not important to the organization. But sometimes you have to start there. If that's the case, strategically recruit people for your team. Like-minded people who have a passion for sustainability are good to include because they will have the energy to see efforts through to completion. But recruit people who have influence as well – formal or informal – and who represent key positions in the organization (e.g. purchasing, facilities, office management and production) and develop them into advocates for the effort.

Table 1.2 *Implementation strategies*

With top management support	Without top management support
Determine the best opportunities.	Find a low-risk, high-potential project.
Communicate with, educate and involve employees.	Gather baseline data.
Form a steering group or management team to oversee the initiative.	Use informal networks and below-the-radar screen funds to conduct the project.
Launch pilot projects.	Document your results in dollars and cents.
	Begin educating executives about sustainability, your successes and latent opportunities.

BOX 1.3 CASE EXAMPLE: HOW *NOT* TO BUILD SUPPORT

One of our clients employed a passionate individual who inadvertently created longstanding ill-will about the company's sustainability effort. He dug through waste cans for recyclable materials and scolded people about their misdeeds. He wrote judgemental emails that were widely circulated. Eventually, he was tackled and muzzled; but his legacy lives on to this day. The moral to this story: make sustainability fun, inspiring and engaging, instead of a guilt-trip downer.

RESOURCES

The following are other useful general resources on implementing sustainability, listed from the most recent to the oldest:

- AtKisson, A. (2008) *The ISIS Agreement*, Earthscan, London
- Blackburn, W. R. (2008) *The Sustainability Handbook*, Earthscan, London
- Epstein, M. (2008) *Making Sustainability Work: Best Practices in Managing and Measuring Corporate Social, Environmental and Economic Impacts*, Greenleaf Publishing, Sheffield, UK
- Axelrod, D. (2007) *How to Get People to Care About What You Find Important*, www.everydayengagement.com
- Hitchcock, D. and Willard, M. (2006) *The Business Guide to Sustainability*, Earthscan, London
- Doppelt, B. (2003) *Leading Change toward Sustainability*, Greenleaf Publishing, Sheffield, UK
- Nattrass, B. and Altomare, M. (2002) *Dancing with the Tiger*, New Society Publishers, Gabriola Island, BC, Canada
- Anderson, L. A. and Anderson, D. (2001) *The Change Leader's Roadmap*, Jossey-Bass/Pfeiffer, San Francisco, CA
- Senge, P. M., Kleiner, A., Roberts, C. and Roth, G. (1999) *The Dance of Change: The Challenges to Sustaining Momentum in Learning Organizations*, Doubleday, New York
- Maurer, R. (1996) *Beyond the Wall of Resistance*, Bard Books, Austin, TX

METHODS AND INSTRUCTIONS

This section of each chapter includes specific and well-tested methods, exercises and tools that you can use within your organization. We provide an overview of the tools, as in Table 1.3. Choose the methods that most interest you and read the instructions which follow.

Table 1.3 *Overview of methods for preparing for change*

Readiness assessment	Use this diagnostic to help you determine whether or not you are ready to take on a significant change effort.
Lesson from the past	Use this to help you identify the change strategies that have worked (or failed) in the past.
Stages of implementation assessment	This assessment is appropriate if you have already begun some efforts or projects.
Champion assessment	Use this to help clarify what will be expected of your effort's champion.
Strategies for system change	Use this more sophisticated approach when you are ready to consider systemic organizational change strategies.

Readiness assessment

When to use. This is best done before starting any serious work on your sustainability plan.

How to prepare. Determine who should participate in this assessment. Ideally you will want some leadership involvement.

How to conduct this activity. Honest answers to these four key questions will form the foundation for all subsequent efforts. So, be honest and thorough!

- How aware and supportive is your organization of sustainability?
- How does sustainability relate to organizational goals, business threats and other priorities?
- How does sustainability relate to past organizational efforts?
- What makes you think this is the right time to move sustainability forward?

How to debrief. Use your answers to design your initial strategy. Are you ready to move forward or is there foundation work that you need to do? Try to connect with or research organizations that have successful sustainability programmes and find out how they were able to build support and relevance.

Lessons from the past

When to use. This exercise can help you to identify organizational change strategies that work best in your organization. It is especially important to do if you have had some memorable failures.

How to prepare. Convene people with enough history or knowledge of past efforts to meaningfully assess them.

How to conduct this activity. Hang two flip charts. Label one 'worked well' and the other 'do differently'. Ask the group you convene to remember and describe past change efforts. These might include quality improvement initiatives, changes to processes or equipment, major lay-offs, etc. For each story or incident that is shared, ask the group to identify what worked well or contributed to the success of the effort and what didn't or should have been handled differently. Collect their comments on the appropriate chart.

How to debrief. Review the two lists together and see if there are any lessons to be gleaned from these past experiences. What will you want to be sure to remember and employ as you pursue your sustainability initiative?

Stages of implementation assessment

When to use. This assessment is appropriate to use when you have already started down the path towards sustainability. It will help you to determine where you are and what strategies will keep you moving along.

How to prepare. Use the statements in each box as a checklist. Determine which list best describes your organization.

How to debrief. Based on where your organization lands, discuss strategies that are most appropriate at that point in time. You may want to discuss past change efforts and what helped them progress from one phase to the next.

Table 1.4 *Stages of implementation*

Incubator phase	Initiative phase	Integrated phase
☐ We have little support from leadership. They may know what we are doing or have done but are not significantly involved themselves. ☐ Our leaders do not have a full understanding of what sustainability is or means to our organization. ☐ We have only implemented one or two small projects. The effort is largely invisible to most of the organization.	☐ We have some management support. ☐ This has become a formal and recognized initiative. ☐ There is an intent to involve the whole organization. ☐ We have some temporary structures in place (e.g. steering committee or green teams) to support the effort.	☐ Many of the efforts, to date, have become integrated within the systems of the organization. (e.g. new employee orientation includes briefing on sustainability; purchasing contracts contain sustainability criteria). ☐ Sustainability is evident in our culture; you see or hear of it everywhere. ☐ Sustainability has become integral to the image of the organization.

Champion assessment

When to use. Use this tool when you have someone in mind for the role of champion. In many cases, but not all, this may be the leader of the organization.

How to prepare. See if your champion is open enough to have the conversation suggested by the items below.

How to conduct this activity. This will best be done in conversation with your champion. Explain to him or her that change efforts benefit from the attention of champions and that this assessment clarifies what is expected of them. Use the assessment in Table 1.5 to ascertain where his or her support gaps might be.

How to debrief. This assessment helps to identify existing strengths and elements that need shoring up. Checking one or two 'nos' on the list is not a deal breaker; but it means that the champion will have to determine either how to compensate or how to work around that potential barrier.

Table 1.5 *Champion assessment*

Organizational perspective	Yes	No
1 Can you clearly and specifically describe the relationship between sustainability and organizational needs/outcomes?		
2 Do you have a compelling need or desire to pursue sustainability?		
3 Do you have a critical mass of stakeholders (informal leaders, union officials, managers, etc.) who will support this change?		
4 Are you able to commit significant resources (time and money) to ensure that the effort will be successful?		
5 Are you willing to accept an initial investment or outlay in exchange for long-term savings?		
6 Are you willing to take some risks and reinvent how your organization operates (e.g. human resource systems and purchasing policies)?		

Personal perspective	Yes	No
1 Do you believe that sustainability is an important issue?		
2 Are you willing to dedicate a significant amount of your time talking about sustainability and ensuring that it is taken seriously?		
3 Do you intend to stay in your position for at least two years until the effort is well established?		
4 Can you take action to ensure that your successor will be equally supportive?		

⤳ Strategies for system change

When to use. Use this more sophisticated approach when you are ready to consider systemic organizational change strategies. This will usually be after you have identified and possibly even implemented a number of sustainability projects.

How to prepare. Several years ago, Donella Meadows, one of the preeminent thinkers of systems theory, wrote a short but seminal article on how to affect change in complex systems. The ideas have a good deal of relevance to the implementation of organizational change. Find a copy of Donella Meadows's article 'Places to Intervene in a System' (*Whole Earth*, winter 1997) and ask the people participating in this activity to read it before the session. Or, if the article is not available, at least circulate the list and description of the nine levers for change described below.

How to conduct this activity:

- Discuss the levers of change that Donella Meadows describes in her article 'Places to Intervene in a System'. It may be necessary to clarify or explain some of them.
- Identify and talk about which (if any) of the levers your sustainability initiative has already used. Are there more ways in which you could use these? Do they tend to be the less effective strategies towards the bottom of Meadows's list (i.e. with higher numbers) or do they tend to be near the top of her list? Why?
- Assuming you haven't used all the levers suggested by Meadows, consider how you might apply the others.
- Spend time talking about what the levers suggest for moving forward, either with your entire sustainability initiative or individual projects.

Table 1.6 *Places to intervene in a system*

Strategy	Example
1 **Change the paradigm.** Create and model the mindset that you want others to assume	Smoking in public: not long ago we accepted smokers as part of public life. Today we look askance at those who light up in public places. Compulsory education: for our generation, it is unthinkable that children should not attend school.
2 **Change the goals of the system.** Establish clear and compelling goals that focus a population on the desired outcome .	Man on the moon: John F. Kennedy set an unthinkable goal and inspired a nation to believe in it. National forest policies: those who manage the national forests on our behalf often feel whip-sawed by the changes in focus issued by the US Congress.

Table 1.6 *Places to intervene in a system* (Cont'd)

Strategy	Example
	One year, their goal is to 'steward' the forest; the next, it is to maximize timber sales. First they were to prevent all fires, then allow fires unless they jeopardized private property.
3 **Enable self-organization.** Recognize the fact that systems have a self-organizing nature and enable and empower those systems to adapt as they need to suit their environments.	Watershed councils: Oregon's watershed councils were granted broad privileges by the federal government for determining how to respond to the US Endangered Species Act while being held accountable for the ultimate results.
4 **Change the rules (incentives, punishments, constraints).** Use laws and rules to encourage the behaviour that you want.	Seat belt laws: these laws have effectively changed driving behaviour among a majority of motorists within one generation. Food stamps: we regulate what food stamps can be used for in an effort to curb alcoholism and smoking. Pollution trading mechanisms: we created rules and values around nitrogen and sulphur oxide (NO_x/SO_x) emissions, in this way fostering a general decline in pollution.
5 **Improve information flows.** Provide information to those who need it to make decisions and take actions.	Nutrition labelling: industry fought it – no one thought it would make a difference. In the end, we find that people do read the labels on food packages and adjust their buying practices accordingly. Posting energy bills: one organization did nothing else in its effort to curb electricity consumption but hang its monthly bills in the elevator. Consumption dropped 20 per cent in the first month. The Global Reporting Initiative and Carbon Disclosure Project: shareholders and consumers put increasing pressure on organizations to publish their policies, practices and accomplishments related to environmental performance and social responsibility.

Table 1.6 *Places to intervene in a system* (Cont'd)

Strategy	Example
6 **Reduce the gains from positive feedback loops.** Introduce strategies that reduce the gain or slow the growth in a positive feedback loop.	Estate taxes: these taxes are designed to prevent the perpetuation of family dynasties created by our 'wealth makes more wealth' economic systems. Campaign finance reform: the more money a candidate raises, the more likely she or he will be elected, which makes it easier to raise more money for the next election and so on.
7 **Regulate negative feedback loops.** Strengthen or introduce appropriately measured negative feedback into a system in order to keep the system within safe bounds and prevent an 'overshoot and collapse' scenario.	Impact taxes: Europe taxes gasoline consumption very heavily in an attempt to curb its consumption. Oregon is considering a 'pay as you drive' auto insurance law that penalizes high-mileage drivers.
8 **Redesign material stocks and flows.** Redesign the infrastructure that dictates how the system operates.	Sustainable forestry practices: this method of managing forests allows logging without depleting the stock of trees. Public transit: statistics indicate that there is a tipping point in mass transit; if it runs often enough and to enough places, people will ride. Trained workforce: education is an investment in human capital stocks that can pay economic *and* social dividends.
9 **Manipulate the numbers.** Adjust the 'faucet' to increase or decrease the flow of stock through the system or change the numbers to shorten the lapse between actions and their consequences.	Energy policy: we shape our future by choosing to favour subsidies for the oil industry over investments in renewable energy sources. Social capital: investing in jails may meet an immediate concern; but investing in health and education may return better results in the long run.

Source: adapted from Meadows (1997)

Refining the Business Case

CONCEPTS AND CASE EXAMPLES

In order for your sustainability effort to be sustainable, you need to have a clear business reason for pursuing it. While pursuing sustainability because 'It's the right thing to do' may be enough to start your effort, eventually you need to get to the place where sustainability is not just nice to have, but crucial to your long-term success. At some point, your executives have to be able to explain – to themselves, their stakeholders and their employees – why this is worth the time, expense and effort.

There are a number of different methods for doing this. Bob Willard, in his book *The Sustainability Advantage* (2002), shows you how to compute the bottom-line benefits of pursuing sustainability, everything from reduced expenses and increased market share to improved employee retention. In some situations, this is a useful exercise. However, a substantial number of organizational change efforts can claim to do many of these same things. You need a compelling reason why sustainability makes more sense than the others.

This approach assumes that making and saving money are the primary reasons for pursuing sustainability. What we've found is that this financial analysis can help to *support* a decision to pursue sustainability; but the reasons for pursuing sustainability are often far more complex. For each organization and each person, you have to find the best hook.

BOX 2.1 CASE EXAMPLE: MAKE SUSTAINABILITY MORE THAN JUST THE 'RIGHT THING TO DO'

We were consulting with a large legal firm that was pursuing sustainability. A few of the partners were on board; but we suspected others saw this as a distraction. When we asked their sustainability steering committee members why they were pursuing sustainability, we were told: 'It's just the right thing to do.' There's nothing wrong with that; it's just not very compelling and is sometimes off-putting to others. It also makes it easy to cut the programme when times get tough or workloads call. So, we started laying out other reasons why sustainability might be strategic to their business – namely:

- Many of their business clients were pursuing sustainability as a strategic initiative. Shouldn't they at least know what their clients were doing so that they could give them good advice?
- Legal firms are in tough competition with each other for top talent. More and more young professionals want to work for organizations that share their values. Instead of just competing on wages, firms are appealing to recruits on the additional basis of their practices.
- Sustainability helps you to understand where the world is headed and attorneys help clients manage risk. Understanding sustainability could help them to show their clients how to avoid future risks, not just the current ones.
- A significant amount of new regulation is coming out of regions such as the European Union. If they had clients with an international business, they ought to know what new regulations were coming down the pipeline.
- Whole new areas of law are emerging from sustainability, including renewable energy, product stewardship and cap-and-trade systems for carbon. Did they want their firm to expand their practice into some of these new areas or cede this ground to their competitors? In fact, they had already created a name for themselves in one of these areas, but hadn't seen the other opportunities.
- Attorneys often create boundaries around what is considered possible. By providing legal advice, they limit action that their clients are willing to take. So, attorneys can inadvertently be a hindrance to progress in society if they don't understand where the world needs to head. For example, in the US, attorneys often give clients who want to create a business several options for organizing, but routinely ignore employee-owned co-operatives.
- Conversely, they can help clients – both business and government – to create policies that circumvent unnecessary roadblocks to progress. For example, the state or city attorney general may provide advice about how to word sustainability-related policies so that they can be implemented.
- In the past, most major social changes were driven by, or at least supported by, lawyers. Think about civil rights and women's rights, along with anti-smoking and drink driving campaigns. Isn't it likely that there will be an important role for attorneys as sustainability unfolds as well? Companies and other entities are already getting sued for their climate impacts. Some believe that climate change will be the next tobacco, a legal battleground.

This conversation helped them to think beyond reducing paper and energy use to see the broader strategic opportunities for their firm. Within six months, the firm was publicly promoting its involvement with sustainability.

Right action, wrong reason?

We don't much care why people want to jump on the sustainability train. Many are motivated by a belief that it's the right thing to do and a reflection of moral values. Others might be worried about their corporate image, changing customer expectations or impending regulations. Some might be interested in specific incentives and financial programmes. Others might be excited about the prospects to profit from the challenges. Usually, businesses get involved because of a complex set of motivations. Don't fall into the trap of wanting people to join for the *right* reasons. Help them to find *their* reasons.

Most of the early adopters pursued sustainability because they had a passion for the issue. As with most movements, that was a small percentage of the population. Now that sustainability is going mainstream, it's easier to convince others to get on board the sustainability train, although the reasons are more diverse. It's okay in our book if clients adopt the sustainability ethos because their customers are demanding it or their competitors are looking good because of it. Once sustainability issues begin to be talked about openly in the organization, you'll be amazed by the heart-felt response from unexpected people.

Box 2.2 Case example: Make sustainability inevitable

We have been most successful with the current wave of sustainability recruits when we can paint sustainability as inevitable. The chief financial officer (CFO) of one of our clients was intrigued with sustainability; but the president of this closely held private business was planning to sell the company in the next few years. He had a short-timer attitude. It was also a small company that, like most, was running flat out just to keep up with orders. How could it be convinced to take time to look at this long-range, strategic issue when it was living day to day?

We asked for a short list of the company's customers and suppliers. With that information, we were able to use the internet to find which of these companies were pursuing sustainability. We knew we'd hit the jackpot when Wal-Mart was on their list of customers. Wal-Mart is famous for leaning on its suppliers and, since 2006, it's been on the sustainability bandwagon, pushing for reductions in packaging, energy use and greenhouse gases.

Our executive briefing was littered with stories from the company's major customers, suppliers and competitors. Suddenly, it looked as if it was falling behind. Pursuing sustainability no longer appeared to be 'fluff'. We told the staff that they could either get their act together before Wal-Mart came knocking or wait and be surprised. Ironically, their first letter from Wal-Mart arrived two weeks later. We didn't have anything to do with it: honest!

Why organizations pursue sustainability

PriceWaterhouse Coopers first did a study in 2002 to find out why businesses were pursuing sustainability. Its early research indicated that most organizations were pursuing sustainability to protect their image. This is one reason why the financial analysis approach is too narrow. Intangible risks are difficult to quantify. What does bad press cost you? How hard is it to attract and retain employees? What disaster might befall you that could expose your vulnerabilities? These risks, these expectations of stakeholders, don't easily show up on a spreadsheet; but they are very real business reasons for pursuing sustainability.

Here's a partial listing of motivations to unearth.

Business reasons:

- *Customers are asking for it.* A sustainability coordinator in a multinational engineering firm began tracking how many times requests for a proposal (RFPs) asked about its environmental management systems and sustainability. This data pushed the firm into the field.
- *First mover advantage.* Often, the first to market with an innovation gets the recognition, while others in the industry may match or surpass their efforts. BP gets most of the attention even though other oil companies have engaged in similar efforts. Interface Carpet gets the glory, while few know about Shaw and C&L Floorcoverings. Some companies and communities recognize the benefit of being known as the first and the best. For example, Portland, Oregon, was featured in a sustainability documentary, in part because it was the first city in the US to have a *Climate Action Plan*.
- *Getting left behind.* It only took a couple of years for LEED to become the *de facto* standard for commercial buildings. Architects who weren't certified have been scrambling to catch up lest they look hopelessly out of touch.
- *Logical extension of existing efforts.* As mentioned in Chapter 1, Cascade Corporation, one of our manufacturing clients, a niche manufacturer with operations in a number of countries, was already pursuing lean manufacturing and employee empowerment strategies. Then its board asked the president to think about social responsibility. Its programmes were starting to feel like a jumble: quality, lean, corporate social responsibility (CSR), ISO 14001 and empowerment. We were able to demonstrate how sustainability could act as a unifying umbrella under which these different efforts could fall.
- *Protecting one's image.* Nike became interested in sustainability after being lambasted for the treatment of workers in its suppliers' operations. It asked the question: what might hit us next? Environmental sustainability was the answer.

Personal reasons:

- *Children*. Perhaps the most common reason people have for an interest in sustainability is their concern for the future of their children or grandchildren. The sustainability director at Norm Thompson, a catalogue retailer, showed pictures of the employees' own children in a kick-off meeting, and there was nary a dry eye in the house!
- *Illness*. Some people have a family member or friend with a disease that is suspected to be related to environmental triggers (e.g. asthma, cancer, autism or non-Hodgkin lymphoma).
- *Love of nature*. Many who enjoy the outdoors may or may not identify themselves as environmentalists (e.g. hunting, fishing, hiking, forestry, etc.).
- *Personal experience*. People may have been the recipient of discrimination or had other experiences that left them feeling empathy for the plight of others.
- *Travel*. Often travellers return home with an appreciation of the world's problems and exposure to different ways of addressing societal challenges.

Find the hook for each person and each organization. Help them to see that their values and their volunteer/charity efforts are part of this larger movement.

BOX 2.3 MAKE THE MESSAGE MEMORABLE

According to the authors of *Made to Stick* (Heath and Heath, 2007), stories can be more compelling than statistics. Stories engage the audience's minds and curiosity. Like Aesop's *Fables*, they provide memorable ways to retain important lessons. Gather stories that help to make important points about sustainability.

People's identity may be more important to their decisions than their own personal self-interest.

RESOURCES

Making the business case

Bob Willard, author of *The Sustainability Advantage* (2002), has excellent resources for calculating and communicating hard-nosed bottom-line benefits. Go to his website to download free worksheets and a slide deck for communicating the business case (see www.sustainabilityadvantage.com/products/index.html). There is also information about his two books and a DVD on how to convince executives about the business case.

METHODS AND INSTRUCTIONS

In this section, we explain three activities or processes that are helpful in developing a business case for sustainability.

Worldwide trend cards

Dorothy Atwood of the Zero Waste Alliance helped to develop this process. See the sample trend cards at the end of this section.

When to use. Many people new to sustainability are oblivious to the trends that have been alarming people in this field. This activity exposes them to these trends and asks them to consider which are most likely to affect them and what they think could or should be done about them.

How to prepare. Select the cards that you want to use. Put the information for each issue on a separate piece of paper and get the most recent and credible chart demonstrating the trend. Be sure to use the most credible sources. Feel free to create your own cards around issues related to your industry or geographic area. See the samples below.

How to conduct the activity. Explain that there are a number of long-term trends that are likely to have widespread effects. Break into small groups (three to four people each) and give each group one or two trend cards. Ask them to read the cards and discuss the implications (for their business or community, as appropriate).

How to debrief. Have each group explain the trend(s) that they were assigned and report on what they felt were the likely impacts upon their community or organization. After all groups have reported, discuss which trends seem the most relevant in your situation.

Table 2.1 *Overview of methods for refining the business case*

Process	When to use
Worldwide trends cards	Familiarize people with the doom-and-gloom trends in the world. This is helpful for people who need a wake-up call because their ignorance of the issues is preventing a sense of urgency. This must be balanced, however, with a hopeful message of things that they can do.
Strengths, weaknesses, opportunities and threats (SWOT)	SWOT helps to organize ideas about an organization's internal and external positives and negatives. It is a common tool for strategic planning.
Long-term sustainability strategy	A sustainability strategy highlights strategies and business models that will be necessary over time.

Climate change

Look at the information below and consider the following questions:

- What is this likely to mean for the world?
- How does this interact with other global trends?
- What is this likely to mean for our area in the long term (within the life of our grandchildren)?

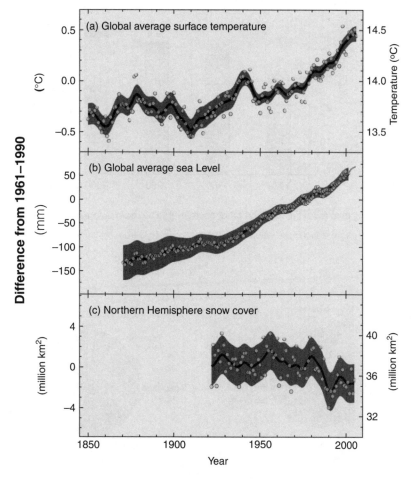

Figure 2.1 *Climate change impacts*

Source: IPCC (2007, Figure 1.1).

- What could we do in our region to deal with these trends (either to adapt and/or to reverse them)?
- What connections do you see between this issue and actions we could or should take in our organization?

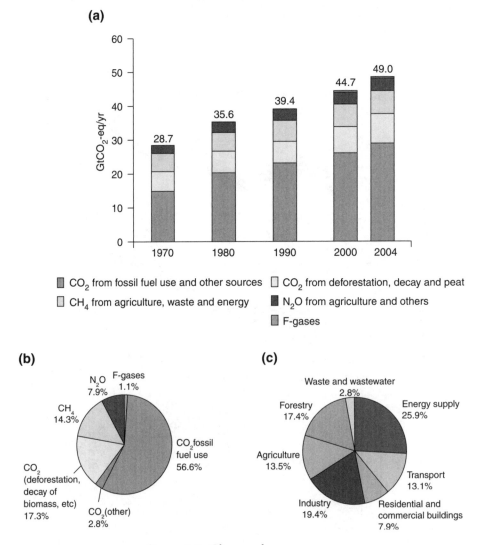

Figure 2.2 *Climate change sources*

Source: IPCC (2007, Figure 2.1).

Water

Look at the information below and consider the following questions:

- What is this likely to mean for the world?
- How does this interact with other global trends?
- What is this likely to mean for our area long term (within the life of our grandchildren)?
- What could we do in our region to deal with these trends (either to adapt and/or to reverse them)?
- What connections do you see between this issue and actions we could or should take in our organization?

Water facts:

- Water withdrawals from rivers and lakes for irrigation, household and industrial use doubled in the last 40 years.
- Humans now use between 40 to 50 per cent of the freshwater running off land to which the majority of the population has access.
- In some regions, including the Middle East and North Africa, humans use 120 per cent of renewable supplies.
- Close to 20 per cent of the world's population lacks access to safe drinking water (1.3 billion people).
- It's not just developing countries. Europe and the US Midwest have nitrate pollution (from fertilizers).
- Water use by category: 69 per cent agriculture; 23 per cent industry; 8 per cent domestic.
- According to the World Resources Institute, water use is growing twice as fast as population.

Source: The Millennium Ecosystem Services Assessment et al (2000).

Body burden

Look at the information below and consider the following questions:

- What is this likely to mean for the world?
- How does this interact with other global trends?
- What is this likely to mean for our area long term (within the life of our grandchildren)?
- What could we do in our region to deal with these trends (either to adapt and/or to reverse them)?
- What connections do you see between this issue and actions we could or should take in our organization?

Body burden facts:

- Women's breast milk around the world is filled with toxic chemicals: pesticides, wood preservatives, industrial solvents, fire retardants, etc., which women then transmit to their babies during breastfeeding.
- Thanks to bio-magnification, breastfed babies ingest 50 times per pound of polychlorinated biphenyls (PCBs) and dioxins than do their parents.
- A 2003 Centers for Disease Control study tested the blood and urine of 2500 anonymous volunteers for 116 chemicals, with positive results found for 89 substances, including PCBs, dioxins, phthalates and pesticides (Centers for Disease Control and Prevention, 2003).
- In 1998, studies of Swedish breast milk showed that levels of flame retardants known as polybrominated diphenyl ethers (PBDEs) were doubling every two to five years.
- A study of 20 first-time mothers commissioned by the Washington-based Environmental Working Group found considerably higher PBDE levels in US women than those recorded in Sweden.
- Metabolic traces of some agricultural pesticides were noticeably higher in Mexican Americans than in African Americans or non-Hispanic whites, including several compounds now banned in the US, including DDT.

Source: Centers for Disease Control and Prevention (2003); Steingraber (2001).

Fisheries

Look at the information below and consider the following questions:

- What is this likely to mean for the world?
- How does this interact with other global trends?
- What is this likely to mean for our area in the long term (within the life of our grandchildren)?
- What could we do in our region to deal with these trends (either to adapt and/or to reverse them)?
- What connections do you see between this issue and actions that we could or should take in our organization?

Fish facts (according to the United Nations Millennium Ecosystem Assessment):

- At least one quarter of marine fish stocks are overharvested.
- The quantity of fish caught by humans was increasing until the 1980s, but now is decreasing due to the shortage of stocks.
- In some seas, the total weight of fish available to capture is less than one hundredth of that caught before industrial fishing operations.
- Inland fisheries have also declined due to overfishing, habitat degradation and water diversion; these are especially important sources of food for the poor.

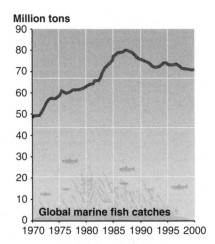

Figure 2.3 *Fisheries*

Source: Millennium Ecosystem Assessment (2005).

Forests
Look at the information below and consider the following questions:

- What is this likely to mean for the world?
- How does this interact with other global trends?

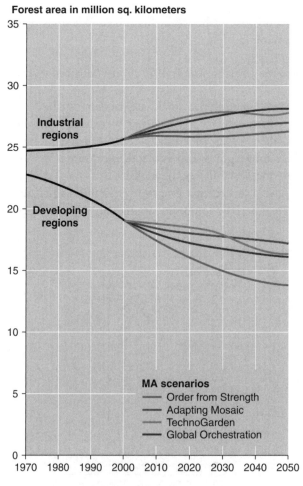

Forest area in million sq. kilometers

Figure 2.4 *Forests*

Source: Millennium Ecosystem Assessment (2005).

- What is this likely to mean for our area in the long term (within the life of our grandchildren)?
- What could we do in our region to deal with these trends (either to adapt and/or to reverse them)?
- What connections do you see between this issue and actions that we could or should take in our organization?

Forest facts

According to a study by the World Resources Institute, almost one half of the Earth's original forest cover is gone and only one fifth of the original cover remains as frontier forests – forests large enough to sustain substantial populations of indigenous species even when faced with natural disasters such as fire and storms (WRI, no date).

Population

Look at the information below and consider the following questions:

- What is this likely to mean for the world?
- How does this interact with other global trends?
- What is this likely to mean for our area in the long term (within the life of our grandchildren)?
- What could we do in our region to deal with these trends (either to adapt and/or to reverse them)?
- What connections do you see between this issue and actions that we could or should take in our organization?

Note: you may be able to get more current projections from the United Nations for your region from this website: http://esa.un.org/unpp/.

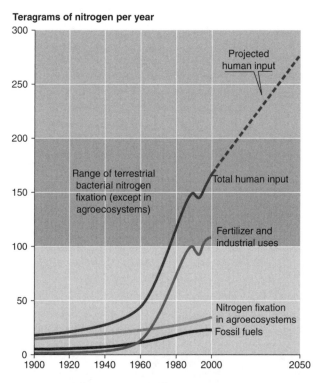

Figure 2.5 *Population projections*

Source: Millennium Ecosystem Assessment (2005).

Nitrogen cycles
Look at the information below and consider the following questions:

- What is this likely to mean for the world?
- How does this interact with other global trends?
- What is this likely to mean for our area in the long term (within the life of our grandchildren)?
- What could we do in our region to deal with these trends (either to adapt and/or to reverse them)?
- What connections do you see between this issue and actions that we could or should take in our organization?

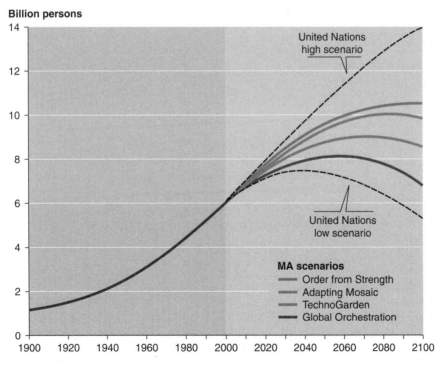

Figure 2.6 *Human impacts on nitrogen*

Source: Millennium Ecosystem Assessment (2005).

Nitrogen facts:

- Humans now produce more biologically usable nitrogen than is produced by all natural processes.
- More than half of all the manufactured nitrogen fertilizer (first produced in 1913) has been applied since 1985.
- The flow of nitrogen into the oceans has doubled since 1860.
- Phosphorous has also increased in soils threefold between 1960 and 1990. The rate has declined a little since then; but phosphorous can remain in the soil for decades.

Extinctions
Look at the information below and consider the following questions:

• What is this likely to mean for the world?
• How does this interact with other global trends?
• What is this likely to mean for our area in the long term (within the life of our grandchildren)?
• What could we do in our region to deal with these trends (either to adapt and/or to reverse them)?
• What connections do you see between this issue and actions that we could or should take in our organization?

According to the *United Nations Millennium Ecosystem Assessment*, the rate at which species are becoming extinct has increased dramatically. Projections show the rate taking a big leap in the next 50 years.

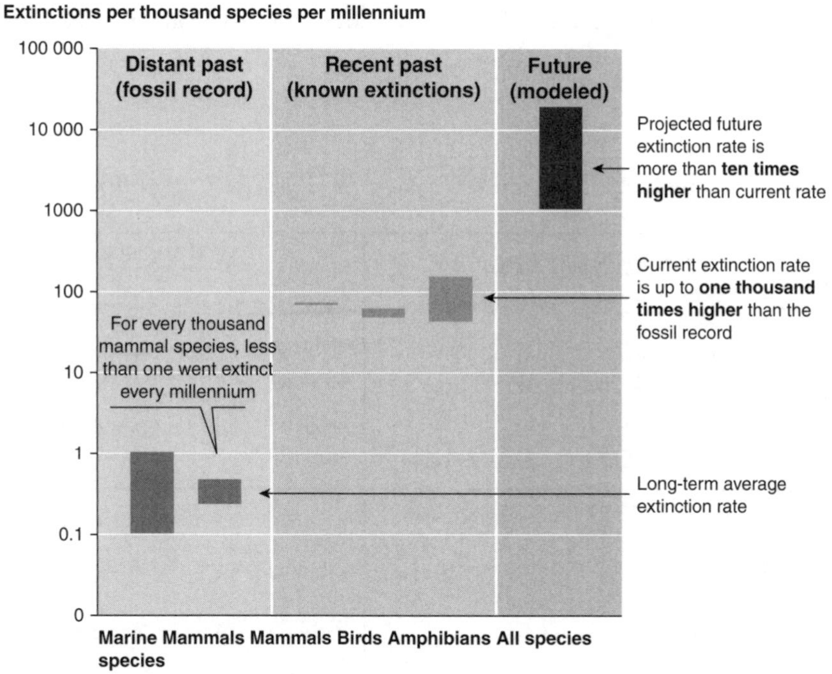

Figure 2.7 *Species extinctions*

Source: Millennium Ecosystem Assessment (2005).

SWOT analysis

When to use. A strengths, weaknesses, opportunities and threats (SWOT) analysis has long been a fixture of strategic planning. Here you consider the SWOT related to sustainability. Use this after familiarizing yourself with sustainability. Then use Table 2.2 to organize your thinking.

How to prepare. Pre-prepare a SWOT flipchart similar to that in Table 2.2.

How to conduct. You can use this diagram to gather information from a general discussion or set up a more formal brainstorming process, such as a nominal group process. Explain the structure of the chart and the terms. Then prompt the group to provide specific examples under each of the four areas.

How to debrief. In general, you want to leverage your strengths, invest in opportunities, divest yourself of, or correct, weaknesses, and manage risks associated with threats. You can develop a strategy around each of the four quadrants (see Table 2.2).

Long-term sustainability strategy

As we indicated in the background reading, it can be instructive to create a vision for three separate timeframes. Use Table 2.3 to prompt ideas and decisions. It may take a year or more to be able to fill in all the boxes.

Table 2.2 *Sample SWOT chart (for a fictional gas utility)*

	STRENGTHS	WEAKNESSES
Internal	Knowledge of the energy industry. Connections/relationships with every business and most homeowners in our territory. Own the infrastructure and delivery system.	Traditional thinking; staid industry. No internal experts on hydrogen economy. No direct influence on fuel cell production.
	OPPORTUNITIES	THREATS
External	Sell methane enriched with hydrogen for fuel cells. Lease, install and maintain fuel cells.	Climate change and awareness of it. Carbon taxes or cap and trade. Supply of natural gas dwindling.
	Positive	*Negative*

Table 2.3 *Strategies for three timeframes (for a fictional oil-drilling operation)*

Near term	Intermediate term	Long term
How are we going to reduce the sustainability impacts of our operations?	What is our unique contribution and role in moving the world towards a sustainable society and what is a viable business model that supports this?	What could our organization's role be in a fully sustainable society?
Conduct a carbon footprint analysis and reduce energy use.	Develop expertise around geothermal industries.	Become a geothermal energy company instead of an oil-drilling company.
Use bio-based lubricants. Analyse fields based on the best carbon return on investment on a full life-cycle basis.	Seek strategic partners to build and maintain geothermal plants.	Drill for geothermal instead of oil and gas and operate geothermal plants.
Eliminate all flaring of natural gas.		

When to use. When an organization is ready to examine long-term implications of sustainability – this requires a willingness or need to 'break' the existing business model. This can be an effective way to get a group to talk about the 'elephant in the room': the unsustainable impacts that their organization causes.

How to prepare. Consider whether this is going to be a threatening or difficult task for the participants. If it is likely to be so, we suggest first doing the exercise for a few other industries in similar situations. For example, a natural gas utility might want to do this for a couple of other extractive industries. Prepare a flip chart similar to that in Table 2.3 with three blocks.

How to conduct this activity:

1   Set the stage and create an openness to participate. Explain that this is a brainstorming-type activity to generate ideas (this reduces defensiveness). Explain the three timeframes and the main tasks associated with each. Emphasize that change is inevitable and that it's better if you anticipate the need to break your own business model than to have competitors do it first. It can help to discuss some of the sea-change events in your organization's history.
2   If you have more than half a dozen people, break the group up into subgroups of four to eight people and ask them to explore how they would answer each of the three questions. Do the near-term first, then the long-term, and do the middle block last.
3   Rotate amongst the groups to make sure that they are deepening their conversations.

How to debrief. Have each group report out. It's often best to get all the near-term ideas on the flipchart from all groups. Then go back and gather the long-term ideas. Finally, get the intermediate-term ideas. Facilitate the free-wheeling conversation that usually ensues as radical ideas generate excitement or reaction. If desired, choose the ideas that generate the most excitement and flesh them out in more detail. What would be necessary to pull this off? What does this imply that you should be doing now? Who could help you?

3

Creating the Vision of Sustainability

CONCEPTS AND CASE EXAMPLES

Until you know where you are going, it will be very difficult to get there. Once you have established the business case for pursuing sustainability, you need to create the vision of what a sustainable version of your organization will look like. The problem is that sustainability can be a confusing and ambiguous term. It seems that the more commonly it is bantered about, the more open to interpretation it becomes. While the most widely accepted definition from the Brundtland report makes intuitive sense to people, there seems to be general confusion when it comes to applying it to individual organizations (WCED, 1987).

BOX 3.1 THE BRUNDTLAND COMMISSION
DEFINITION OF SUSTAINABILITY

The Brundtland Commission, officially known as the World Commission on Environment and Development (WCED), but more commonly referred to by the name of its chair, Gro Harlem Brundtland, was convened by the United Nations in 1983. The commission was created to address a growing concern about the accelerating deterioration of the environment and the consequences of that deterioration on economic and social development. The report generated by the commission contains the most frequently quoted definition of sustainability: 'Meeting the needs of the present generation without compromising the ability of future generations to meet their needs' (WCED, 1987).

Until the members of your organization have a common understanding of what you are trying to achieve, it will be very difficult to move your organization forward with a concerted effort. It is important, then, to begin your initiative with the selection or creation of a framework for sustainability – something that will define sustainability in meaningful and actionable terms and help you to establish a shared vision of what you are trying to achieve. Specifically, a framework should fulfil these five needs:

1   Provide a common language. You will certainly want everyone in the organization to understand the terms, concepts and the nuances involved in sustainable business practices.
2   Inspire a future vision. Your framework will also help you to craft a vision for what your organization will look like in a sustainable future: what it will be doing and not doing, how it will be relating to its industry and community, and how its business model might change.
3   Suggest standards and/or guidelines. A good framework will provide you with standards and principles that help you to translate the concept of sustainability into actionable ideas. The best ones help define what 'there' looks like and give you standards against which you can measure your progress.
4   Outline priorities and approaches. While it is not always the case, many frameworks also outline strategies for progressing towards sustainability that will make an important contribution to the challenging task of prioritizing and scheduling your activities.
5   Suggest metrics. Ultimately, you will want a set of high-level measures that will help you to track your progress. A good vision should help you know what to measure.

The plethora of sustainability frameworks, guidelines, checklists and tools contribute to the general confusion about sustainability. While the intentions have been good, the resulting laundry list has only made it more difficult to share mental models and communicate. Unfortunately, when fields are new, there tends to be an explosion of approaches that coalesce over time.

BOX 3.2 COMMON SUSTAINABILITY FRAMEWORKS AND TERMS

Frameworks include:

- The Natural Step;
- triple bottom line (sometimes referred to as economy, environment and community)/three Es (economy, environment and social equity);
- corporate social responsibility (CSR)
- Herman Daly's triangle.

Principles comprise:

- *Earth Charter*;
- Caux Roundtable for Business;
- Caux Roundtable for Government;
- *Talloires Declaration*;
- United Nations Global Compact;
- *Equator Principles*;
- *Hannover Principles*;
- Agenda 21;
- precautionary principle;
- product stewardship/extended producer (or product) responsibility (EPR)
- biomimicry;
- natural capitalism;
- industrial ecology;
- smart growth (as in urban planning);
- Coalition for Environmentally Responsible Economies (CERES)
- United Nations Millennium Development Goals (MDGs).

Sector-specific standards, certification and eco-labelling are represented by:

- Leadership in Energy and Environmental Design (LEED);
- Food Alliance;
- organic farming/produce;
- biodynamics;
- Forest Stewardship Council;
- Sustainable Forestry Initiative (SFI);
- Marine Stewardship Council;
- Green Seal;
- Electronic Product Environmental Assessment Tool (EPEAT);
- environmental management systems/ISO 14000;
- Social Responsibility ISO 26000;
- Social Accountability (SA) 8000
- AccountAbility (AA) 1000
- energy-using products (EuP);
- Waste Electrical and Electronic Equipment Directive (WEEE);
- Registration, Evaluation, Authorization and Restriction of Chemicals (REACH);
- European Union Restriction of Hazardous Substances Directive (RoHS);
- Green Globe.

Analytical strategies include:

- life-cycle assessment;
- life-cycle costing;

- design for environment or eco-design;
- total cost assessment;
- ecological footprint;
- conservation economy.

Reporting and measurement/metric tools comprise:

- Global Reporting Initiative (GRI);
- Genuine Progress Indicator;
- World Business Council on Sustainable Development (WBCSD) Greenhouse Gas Protocol.

Hierarchy of frameworks and tools

To help make sense of these frameworks, we've organized them into a hierarchy. Each level in the hierarchy serves a different function and each has its strengths and weaknesses with regard to its use as an organizing structure or set of principles.

Laws of nature. At the top of the hierarchy are the immutable laws that nature imposes on us. They are unalterable and impossible to ignore. Gravity is a good example. It's economically inconvenient when you think about it. Consider how much cheaper construction would be if our designs for buildings and bridges didn't have to account for it. And air transportation would be a snap! No one is dumb enough to ignore this

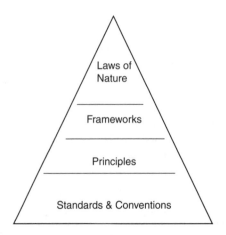

Figure 3.1 *Hierarchy of sustainability models*

particular law, however, probably because the consequences of doing so are immediately felt. But we have chosen to ignore many of the other laws of nature as if they didn't apply to us. We pretend, for instance, that many of the laws of thermodynamics don't matter and that we can continue to use natural resources as if they are limitless (Law of Conservation of Mass and Energy) or throw toxins into our water bodies as if they will flow away and never come back (Law of Entropy). While we would all benefit from a better understanding of these laws, the sophistication of the science necessary makes them a bit unapproachable and difficult to interpret when it comes to making business decisions.

In addition to the laws that govern our physical environment, there are also laws of 'human' nature. These form the basis of human behaviour. While people are influenced by their cultures and locations, there is believed to be a common set of human needs that cuts across race, gender and geography. These human needs are in-born requirements that must be satisfied in order for people to remain healthy – physically, mentally and socially. When these basic needs are not met, our societies and economies become unsustainable. Manfred Max-Neef has perhaps done the best job of summarizing these needs by examining cultures around the world and identifying nine fundamental human requirements: subsistence; protection; affection; understanding; participation; recreation; creation; identity; and freedom. As with the physical laws of nature, we have discovered the unpleasant and often dangerous consequences of ignoring these basic social requirements.

A number of sustainability books refer to Max-Neef's work, including:

- Anielski, M. (2007) *The Economics of Happiness: Building Genuine Wealth*, New Society Publishers, Gabriola Island, BC, Canada
- Hallsmith, G. (2003) *The Key to Sustainable Cities: Meeting Human Needs, Transforming Community Systems*, New Society Publishers, Gabriola Island, BC, Canada

Frameworks. Several conceptual frameworks have emerged to help us translate the laws of nature into understandable rules or constructs. Perhaps the clearest among them is The Natural Step framework that posits four system conditions that define the rules by which we need to live in order to be sustainable. They are written like commandments in that they describe the actions that we must not continue to do. They also benefit from scientific scrutiny, having been vetted by a rigorous process of scientific peer review. Organizations can fairly easily compare their processes and practices to the four system conditions and see specifically where they are with regards to violation.

Similarly comprehensive, though not as thoroughly supported by science, are the frameworks based on the popular triple bottom line: social, economic and environmental health. We have found that talking about sustainability from this frame makes intuitive sense to businesses and gives a specific and reassuring nod to the importance of economic viability to the concept of sustainability.

Principles. The next level in the hierarchy contains a large collection of guidelines that have attempted to specify the actions needed in individual industries or sectors. These are an additional step removed from the laws of nature because they are someone's interpretation of what should be done. They have the benefit of being easy to understand and specific to particular situations, but suffer from the dilution of interpretation. Sustainability is a systems issue and it is easy to get tunnelled into a few key issues, running the risk of missing the comprehensive picture.

Standards and constructs. At the bottom of the hierarchy are the tools and strategies that are very useful when it comes to implementation. Included here are the standards against which industries can compare themselves (e.g. the organic standard for agriculture) and tools that help resolve specific problems (e.g. life-cycle assessments to help businesses root out the sources of pollution and waste). We also include reporting protocols (e.g. the Global Reporting Initiative) that provide specific directives to organizations. While they make an important and useful contribution, used in isolation they can contribute to a myopic approach to sustainability and obscure the big picture entirely.

BOX 3.3 THREE APPROACHES TO DEFINING SUSTAINABILITY

There is no one right framework or set of principles with regards to sustainability; but there are those that are more or less appropriate or relevant to your organization. The three case studies that follow illustrate how organizations develop hybrid versions that fit their own cultures.

SERA Architects in Portland, Oregon, was an early convert to sustainability. It began its journey through its exposure to The Natural Step. While the framework seemed to fit the company's needs generally, it adapted the language of the system conditions to speak more meaningfully to its employees. SERA Architects now define the four rules by which it operates as:

1   *Choose*: are the choices I make fair and equitable?
2   *Take*: can the Earth replace what I take?
3   *Make*: am I poisoning the Earth, water or air?
4   *Respect*: do I respect the biodiversity of flora and fauna?

The Oregon Museum of Science and Industry liked The Natural Step, as well. As a science museum, the notions of the systems conditions spoke to the science mindset of the organization. It didn't feel, however, that the four system conditions represented a balanced set of principles and therefore married the TNS framework with the triple bottom line framework. The museum uses three of the four system conditions as part of the way in which it defines its environmental vision for the organization, but specifically added elements to the social realm and included explicit mention of the economic to ensure that it didn't lose focus on its mission to educate and the need to stay financially stable. We encouraged the museum to identify both internal and external elements within the triple bottom line. Otherwise, the economy often becomes interpreted narrowly as profitability, ignoring other positive economic impacts that the organization can have on the community in terms of jobs, new industry clusters and local purchasing. Table 3.1 shows common metrics if you merge the triple bottom line and The Natural Step.

Table 3.1 *The Natural Step imbedded in the triple bottom line*

	Social	Economic	Environmental
Internal	Employee satisfaction	Financial stability/ profits	Energy efficiency Zero waste Low toxicity
External	TNS system condition 4: human needs	Sustainable economic development Local purchasing	TNS system conditions 1 to 3: climate neutral Zero toxic emissions Sourcing from sustainable stocks

Stonyfield Farms, which makes yogurt in New Hampshire, is an organization that was founded on socially responsible principles. For them, sustainability didn't feel like something new or different, just another way to express what they have been about all along. The logical framework for them was to use their existing mission and values statements, adjusting the language to ensure that they included the nuances of sustainability.

Stonyfield Farms' Mission Statement:

- Produce the very highest quality all natural and certified organic products that taste incredible.
- Educate consumers and producers about the value of protecting the environment and of supporting family farmers and sustainable farming methods.
- Serve as a model that environmentally and socially responsible businesses can also be profitable.
- Provide a healthful, productive and enjoyable workplace for all employees, with opportunities to gain new skills and advance personal career goals.
- Recognize our obligations to stockholders and lenders by providing an excellent return on their investment (Gray and Balmer, 2004).

This mission has been honed to three principles: healthy food, healthy people and healthy planet. Stonyfield developed metrics to track its impacts upon all of these areas.

Long-term visioning

While there are many current and urgent issues (such as climate change) that may attract our immediate attention, sustainability requires systems thinking and keeping the long term in view. Considering too short a perspective leads us to implement strategies that are equivalent to rearranging the deck chairs on the *Titanic*. Once organizations understand sustainability and all that it entails, we present three different timeframes and ask them to grapple with the implications of each.

Near term. This is where most organizations start (and, unfortunately, sometimes end). In this perspective, organizations hold their current practices up to their chosen framework and determine where they are out of alignment. This process (as described in more detail in Chapter 4) focuses primarily on the near term by assessing major impacts and identifying priorities for immediate action. While this is critical and necessary work, it's important to remember that in the big picture it is likely insufficient. After all, doing the unsustainable thing more efficiently won't get us to sustainability.

Long term. At some point, every organization should grapple with its business model. People begin to see what it *really* means to be fully sustainable and this often requires major changes to the business model. As we tell our clients, better that you break your own business model in a planned way than have someone else do it for you! For most organizations, this vision won't easily be attained for a decade or more. But the vision begs the questions: is what the organization does fundamentally sustainable? Is there a place for this product or service in a sustainable world? What will be the role of this organization in a sustainable society? The answers may suggest a radically new business model. No organization likes to think of itself as a dinosaur; but sustainability will upend many of our existing markets.

The transition. The space between the immediate situation and the sustainable future in which the organization's model could be in jeopardy is the area where real strategic planning takes place. This step contains the path forward: the connection between the existing business model and the one that fits a sustainable world. Later in this chapter we provide an exercise for navigating this transition and increasing the likelihood that the organization will have a place in our future (see also 'Long-term sustainability strategy' in Chapter 2).

BOX 3.4 NW NATURAL TAKES ON CLIMATE CHANGE

Of all the industries that would want to take a see-no-evil approach to climate change, natural gas utilities would have to be near the top of the list. Unlike electric utilities or combined electricity and gas utilities, they can't tout wind power or solar. But one of our clients, NW Natural, a natural gas utility, looked at its long-term vision and was brave enough to confront the fact that it sells a greenhouse gas (methane) for a living. Exploring that dilemma openly, talking about it with employees, has unleashed a wave of excitement and innovation. It seems that employees are relieved to have the topic out in the open and are eager to help find solutions. They are working to track the carbon dioxide (CO_2) associated with the company's operations and are developing programmes to reduce the climate impacts of their core product.

Like BP in the oil industry, NW Natural led natural gas utilities in the US to deal publicly with climate change. It catalysed a trend among natural gas utilities to decouple rates from usage, enabling them to promote energy efficiency without hurting their bottom line. NW Natural, then, was the first stand-alone natural gas utility to offer a carbon product: Smart Energy allows customers to offset the emissions associated with their gas use while helping to promote the use of biodigesters on dairy farms. Its nickname is cow power.

NW Natural has developed a nuanced intermediate strategy that helps its bottom line. Natural gas is the cleanest of the fossil fuels; in addition, when fuel is used at the source rather than to generate electricity, customers can reduce their greenhouse gas emissions by over 20 per cent. Its ad campaign, which explains these concepts, has received national recognition. Its efforts to help its customers use less and then to offset what remains, using its Smart Energy programme, puts it in a conversation with its customers about efforts to reduce their carbon footprint. NW Natural has not yet figured out what variety of businesses it will be in long term; but it reminded its employees how many different businesses it's been in its 148-year history, so it has confidence that it can find a way forward. It knows its current business model is unsustainable, but is eager to reinvent itself once again.

Tips for establishing a vision

- If the list of framework options is too daunting to examine, consider basing your conversation on the three most commonly used frameworks: triple bottom line, The Natural Step or the Global Reporting Initiative (GRI). Many of our clients end up using one or some combination of these three. The GRI is particularly relevant to large international organizations that will be expected, at some point, to produce a sustainability report for international audiences. The Natural Step is effective at translating the science of sustainability into concepts that people understand, but admittedly appears to be weighted towards environmental considerations.
- However you go about defining sustainability for your organization, be sure to maintain a systems perspective and don't fall prey to 'tunnel' vision. It's easy to get caught up in one or two important sustainability issues (e.g. climate change); but sustainability is about more than the issue *du jour*. Make sure that you address the full definition of sustainability and that you give equal weight to the three areas of consideration: economic sustainability, environmental sustainability and social sustainability. Trading any one off for the other two violates the basic premise behind the concept.

- Imagining a sustainable version of your organization can frequently seem fantastic. Don't let the seemingly impossible task of achieving true sustainability deter you from putting the necessary dramatic stake in the ground. You can be honest – that the vision is likely in the distant future (15 to 20 years); but it is critical to set the target high because that's what it will take. We are all a long way from sustainability now; but what's the alternative? We have to shoot high.
- Postpone the new business model conversation. Asking people to think about the fundamental premises of their businesses is daunting and often literally unthinkable at first. Eventually, once people come to truly understand sustainability, it becomes impossible to ignore and much easier to imagine.

Box 3.5 Fort Lewis Army Base
and big, hairy audacious goals (BHAGs)

Fort Lewis Army Base in Washington State assembled a broad group of stakeholders to help them set goals related to sustainability as part of their environmental management system. What resulted were ambitious big, hairy audacious goals (BHAGs) grounded in natural laws: create zero net waste, recover all listed and candidate endangered species in the South Puget Sound region, reduce potable water use by 75 per cent and contribute zero pollutants to groundwater. Their sustainability programme has saved them over US$1 million dollars in direct cost savings or cost avoidance. They have also eliminated 89 tonnes of hazardous material and reduced their greenhouse gas emissions by 78 tonnes. Their forestland is now certified as sustainable by the Forest Stewardship Council.

Source: Hitchcock and Willard (2006)

Box 3.6 Hawaii 2050 Sustainability Plan

In 2007, Hawaii engaged its community in a long-range planning process involving over 10,000 residents. The process included web surveys, community meetings, public opinion polling and opportunities for youth involvement. Involving the public so extensively was time consuming and created a lot of work, but was worth it in the end. All of this public input is what makes the document alive. The final plan includes a list of nine priority actions with interim benchmark goals. At the time of writing, the plan is going through the legislative process to be codified into law and to create a sustainability council to ensure accountability. You can learn more about Hawaii's plan and approach at www.hawaii2050.org.

RESOURCES

Please see Appendix A of our last book, *The Business Guide to Sustainability* (Hitchcock and Willard, 2006) for a listing of common sustainability frameworks and when they are most useful. In addition, these resources may be helpful:

- Cook, D. (2004) *The Natural Step: Towards a Sustainable Society*, Green Books, Bristol, UK;
- Edwards, A. R. (2005) *The Sustainability Revolution: Portrait of a Paradigm Shift*, New Society Publishers, Gabriola Island, BC, Canada;
- EPA (2007). 'State of the Environment (SoE) reporting frameworks', Environmental Protection Agency of South Australia, www.epa.sa.gov.au/soe_frame.html, accessed 26 August 2008.
- Robert, K. H., Schmidt-Blee, B., Aloisi de Larderel, J., Basile, G., Jansen, J. L., Keuhr, R., Price Thomas, P., Suzuki, M., Hawken, P. and Wackernagel, M. (2002) 'Strategic sustainable development: Selection, design and synergies of applied tools', *Journal of Cleaner Production*, vol 10, pp197–214.

METHODS AND INSTRUCTIONS

In this section, we explain four processes that can help you to clarify your vision for sustainability (see Table 3.2).

Framework-based visioning

When to use. This simple approach would be best if you have landed squarely on a clearly defined framework. If the framework by itself inspires a clear picture or definition, this exercise could quickly get you to the vision you need.

How to prepare. Make sure that the people participating in this process have a clear and shared understanding of sustainability and the framework that you have chosen. This might require conducting a briefing or training session in advance of implementing the activity.

How to conduct this activity:

1 Explain the framework that you have chosen for your organization.
2 Examine the model and add any criteria, issues or priorities that are relevant to your organization or your situation. What criteria define sustainability for your organization? Are there social/environmental/economic issues that have special

Table 3.2 *Overview of methods for creating the vision*

Process	When to use
Framework-based visioning	This simple approach would be best if you have landed squarely on a clearly defined framework. If the framework by itself inspires a clear picture or definition, this exercise could quickly get you to the vision you need.
Threats and opportunities	Use this approach if you feel you might have trouble getting your colleagues to 'think outside of the box' and be truly creative and open to new ways of thinking about the organization.
Backcasting	Often part of The Natural Step framework, backcasting is useful for organizations that are ready to challenge their business model. Its strength is in defining the 'end game' so that you can more clearly distinguish between decisions that lead to greater possibilities versus those that lead to dead ends.
New business model	This activity is appropriate to use when you are ready to consider the possibility of a radically different future. Often, organizations find this too daunting to do at the very beginning; but at some point it may be necessary to consider a future in which your current business changes significantly.

relevance or priority for your industry or business? Does the framework sufficiently reflect the values of your organization?

3   Test the model/definition. Does it address all three aspects of sustainability? Are they appropriately or evenly weighted?

4   Consider the implications of the framework to your organization both in terms of its internal operations and its relationship with the external world, including your customers, your community and your other key stakeholders. Ask what your organization will necessarily look like in 20 years when it is in complete alignment with the framework. What will you be doing and not doing?

5   What do your answers to the previous set of questions imply about metrics you will track to determine your progress towards this vision?

Threats and opportunities

When to use. People often have difficulty thinking creatively about their own organizations. This activity loosens people up by asking them to examine the threats and opportunities for other businesses first. If you include examples of businesses important to your region or supply chain, it can have the added benefit of examining trends that might indirectly affect your operation.

How to prepare. Make duplicates of the worksheet and put different organization or industry names at the top of each form. Choose industries that are important to your region or operation and ones that allow you to make certain points. For example, when doing this with a natural gas utility, we included a number of extractive industries. If the organization is not likely to be familiar to the audience, explain it as we have in this example. We typically use a company from high-tech, food service, retail, transportation and agriculture. The worksheets are based on The Natural Step framework, so you may want to change the questions if you choose another framework.

How to conduct the activity. If needed, remind the audience of The Natural Step's system conditions (or whatever framework you have chosen). Break people into small groups (four to six people each) and give each group a worksheet. Go over the instructions and give them approximately 15 minutes to work through the questions. You may want to do this in two rounds. First, use the worksheets for other organizations and then do the same process for your own.

How to debrief the activity. Ask each group (or several groups if you don't have time to do them all) to report on their biggest sustainability issue and best sustainability opportunities (one to three). If needed, stretch their thinking by engaging others in the audience. For example, with an extractive industry such as oil drilling, we often explain that your core competence is the ability to find special geological features and then drill really long holes to reach them. How else might you use this core competency to support rather than detract from sustainability? Answers often include developing expertise in geothermal energy and carbon sequestration. Often, if you engage the whole audience, you can quickly generate a handful of possible new business models for each organization. This is empowering: it leaves the audience with the impression that if they can come up with viable models for all of these other businesses, perhaps they can do it for themselves.

Based on your discussion of the questions in Table 3.3:

- What are the two most pressing sustainability issues facing this organization (in other words, what is the funnel wall going to look like for them)?
- What are the two most intriguing business opportunities that relate to sustainability?

Backcasting

When to use. Backcasting is a rigorous process that returns a well-tested approach to sustainability.

Table 3.3 *Sample threats and opportunities worksheet from Veco (an engineering firm involved in oil and natural gas exploration projects)*

System condition 1: from the crust	How dependent is this organization upon fossil fuels or other materials from the Earth's crust?
	How might climate change, or our response to it, affect this organization?
System condition 2: human-made substances	In what ways is this organization dependent upon toxic chemicals? What other human-made substances are important to its success?
System condition 3: productivity of nature	What natural resources are important to this organization? What is the current and likely future status of those resources?
System condition 4: human needs	What are the unintended human side effects from this organization (internally, nationally and internationally? In what ways might this organization be affected by current and future social challenges (e.g. aging of the population, population growth and poverty)?

How to prepare. Where possible, gather rough data that you might have about the organization's current impacts. For example, purchasing records indicate general consumption of materials and utility bills, and travel records indicate energy consumption.

How to conduct this activity. Backcasting is generally associated with The Natural Step process, where it is often referred to as the ABCD process. Instead of forecasting from the current state, backcasting involves envisioning a fully sustainable future and then working backwards to get to that positive future. The four steps in the ABCD process are:

1   *Awareness*: provide training and education about sustainability and The Natural Step framework.
2   *Baseline mapping*: map the organization's 'violations of the system conditions'. The simplest way to do this is to create a flip chart for each of the four system conditions and ask: 'In what ways are we not living up to this rule yet?'
3   *Create a vision*: describe the organization in a fully sustainable state, not worrying about the technology or cost to get there.
4   *Down to action*: work back from the vision to define the incremental steps needed to get there.

There are typically a number of steps and different processes that people use to do this backcasting process and, to some degree, they overlap with other steps in this book. Rather than duplicate all of the material here, we refer you instead to the organization itself: www.naturalstep.org.

New business models

When to use. Use this approach when your organization is ready to consider the far-reaching impacts of sustainability and think creatively and openly about radically different business models.

How to prepare. Where possible, research other organizations in different industries that have made dramatic changes to their business models to share as examples.

How to conduct this activity. We suggest basing this planning process on three critical questions:

1 What are the relevant trends that are likely to impact upon the organization's viability? Climate change, resource depletion and carbon-related regulation, for example, will all have tremendous impacts upon the gas utility mentioned above (see Table 3.3). All three of these trends have sufficient momentum behind them that are unlikely to dissipate in the next decade. The utility's job is to play these trends out and identify the threats and opportunities that they present, individually and collectively.

2 What are the organization's core competencies? This assessment is intended to reveal the assets that the organization has which it can leverage. For the utility mentioned (see Table 3.3), these assets include a mature gas distribution infrastructure, a loyal customer base and a solid hold on its niche in the energy market.

3 What is the sustainable intersection between the competencies and the trends? An organization needs to discover a path between the current state and a sustainable future that leverages its assets and aligns with the conditions of a sustainable world. Our utility, for example, is in a good position to lease home fuel cells, which will likely be fuelled by natural gas (at least in the near future). This business model creates a path that leverages its competencies while evolving the business to one that has a solid footing in a sustainable economy.

In order to help people with this last step, introduce them to four different strategies that might inspire new ideas:

1 *Product-to-service migration.* If you are an organization that produces a tangible product, ask people to consider how that might be transformed into a service. For example, Interface Carpet realized that people don't really want to own carpet. What they want is a comfortable and attractive surface on which to walk. This framing

helped them to create their carpet leasing programme in which they install and service carpet tiles in their customers' buildings. Since the goal is to maximize the life of the carpet rather than encourage customers to replace their carpets frequently with new ones, the company minimizes its consumption of materials while still maintaining a profitable business model.

2   *Cradle-to-cradle design or strategies*. Ask people to consider how their product or service might look or operate if it were part of a continuous loop of consumption. Your product or service would never end up in or contribute to the creation of waste as we know it and would make the fullest and most efficient use of materials already abundantly available in our biosphere.

3   *Biomimicry*. Ask your participants to consider how nature would run your business. If you were forced to mimic natural cycles and technologies, what would it look like?

4   *Regeneration and restoration*. Eventually being truly sustainable is not about being less bad. Ask your participants to consider how they might go about sustaining the economic success of the organization, while at the same time *adding* value to the natural systems.

Identifying Impacts and Priorities

CONCEPTS AND CASE EXAMPLES

Chapter 3 coached you through the creation of a vision for a sustainable version of your organization. Once you are clear about where you are going – your goal state – you will need to take stock of how close or far you are from that vision. This taking stock, which we call an impact assessment, examines the relationship that your organization has with the environment, the society within which it operates, your suppliers, customers and other members of your industry. In short, it is an examination of what you take from the environment and society, what you do with what you take, and what you contribute in the end (both good and bad) to the environment, society and your industry.

Some organizations, especially those in the service or non-profit sector, don't often think of themselves as having environmental or social impacts. After all, there are no belching smoke stacks on top of their offices, no trucks unloading precious resources at their doors, nor any raggedly dressed children working in the back office. Nonetheless, conducting an impact assessment, even on a service organization, can be very revealing. Every organization, for instance, makes use of energy and materials, moves documents and people and makes choices that have rippling effects beyond their office doors. Service organizations, in particular, shape the behaviour of the customers whom they serve. Insurance companies, for example, may not be the biggest consumers of natural resources, but they have a huge impact upon how sustainably their customers behave. They influence whether people locate homes in floodplains or fire zones, what kinds of cars people choose to drive and how they drive them, and what health-impacting lifestyle choices they make. All service-sector businesses (e.g. banks, architects, restaurants and law firms) influence the behaviour and choices of their customers and can, through their own practices and policies, determine whether or not people make more sustainable choices.

In addition, every organization participates in an industry sector (e.g. manufacturing, government, service and high tech). Many of its impacts are determined by the conventions and practices inherent to that industry. In addition to cleaning up its own act and helping its customers to behave more sustainably, an organization should consider how it can influence its industry to bring policies, practices and, where appropriate, legislation, into alignment with the principles of sustainability. As an example, we discovered a law firm in New York City that was operating virtually without paper. This was only possible because conventions had evolved in their area of law to allow electronic signatures on binding contracts. If the profession truly wants to move towards paperless operations, then it will have to negotiate similar agreements across all the fields of law.

Multilevel approach to analysing impacts

An impact analysis can be done at several levels. If you are just beginning the process, we recommend starting with one of the high-level processes described below. These macro-level assessments take a broad look at your operations and identify the major categories of impacts. Once this is done, you will have a better idea of where you need to drill down a level to gather more specific data to support the educated guesses you make at the higher level, or gather baseline data in preparation for action items. As your sustainability efforts mature, you may find it useful or necessary to conduct a detailed life-cycle assessment of one or more of the products that you make or use. This level of analysis can give you the information you need to make choices for material procurement or product/service design.

Look beyond the obvious

Sometimes an activity has more of an impact than is immediately apparent. One of our clients, another legal firm, understood that it was a big consumer of paper (in fact, if you stacked the reams it used each year, the stack would be as tall as a 22-storey skyscraper!). It knew that paper consumption was one impact it could reduce through a variety of changes in employees' work habits. Upon further investigation, however, it began to realize that saving paper was just the tip of the benefits iceberg. In addition to saving an estimated US$20,000 on paper purchases each year, the firm discovered that by migrating to electronic file management, it would save on rent (file cabinets take up a good deal of valuable real estate), support time (all of the staff hours dedicated to retrieving and re-filing documents after they passed through attorney hands) and process inefficiency (by working electronically, a file never got lost or was unavailable because it was checked out by a single person; in fact, multiple people could simultaneously work on an electronic file, magnifying everyone's productivity).

Reveal new sources of process inefficiency

Viewing activities through the lens of sustainability also reveals waste that has gone unnoticed. An engineering firm also sought to reduce its paper consumption. When it examined its processes, it discovered that most of the printing was done in association with the creation of 'check sets' – sets of documents that were printed for quality checks. Some projects went through as many as 35 check sets before the project was completed. This represented more than a waste of paper: it represented a process flaw and a lack of standardization around the points where it was necessary to check for accuracy. By establishing project conventions, the firm could save a good deal of billable staff time as well as paper by systematizing the process.

Go beyond your gates

When assessing their footprints, organizations often overlook the impact of their products after they are shipped to customers. In many cases, use and disposal of products dwarf manufacturing impacts. Electrolux, maker of home appliances, discovered this when conducting a life-cycle analysis of its washing machines. The biggest impact was not in production or delivery, but in the millions of gallons of water – much of it hot – that their machines used during their lifetime. While at first it may seem as if you don't have control over how customers use your products, you actually have two opportunities to influence them. Consider the informational, educational or marketing strategies used by many manufacturers to influence the behaviour of their customers. For example, Charmin toilet paper uses its TV ad campaign to demonstrate (delicately, with animation) that it takes fewer sheets of its product than competitors to 'get the job done'. Every communication you have with a customer (through instructions, marketing, advertising, etc.) is an opportunity to help them make best use of your product.

The biggest opportunity to diminish a product's impact, however, is in design. Electrolux's recognition of its washers' impact led it to innovate its designs in order to create machines that use significantly less water. Not only did this reduce the product's environmental footprint, but gave it a tremendous market advantage. Similarly, Nature Works, the Cargill subsidiary that makes polylactic acid (PLA) plastic, not only designed its product to make use of organic materials instead of petroleum, but can make much of the fact that unlike traditional plastic, its product will biodegrade.

Tips for getting the most out of your impact analysis

- Involve a broad enough group of people in this process that you have all the major functions and operations of your organization represented. This will enable you to identify the most informed and comprehensive list of impacts. At a minimum, consider involving whomever manages your purchasing function, your facilities, your core manufacturing or service delivery operations, and your shipping and receiving.
- Use the framework you employed to create your vision to help you set the criteria for how each aspect of your operation *should* operate. In other words, translate your vision

into the specific actions and materials that your organization will need to employ in order to be sustainable.

- You will also need to decide how much of your organization to analyse: just your facility; just manufacturing or the office; the entire organization? If you choose to address your entire life cycle, you will necessarily have to consider customers and suppliers as well.
- Use existing data where you have it to inform your analysis. Purchasing records, for example, provide a rich source of information about consumption. If your records are not easily sorted by purchase types, ask your key vendors to provide summaries of your purchases for the year. If you reimburse employees for work-related trips, then you likely have a record of transportation energy consumption related to plane and car trips.

RESOURCES

Reporting and metrics

- The International Society of Sustainability Professionals has a webinar recording on *Mapping Your Impacts* that provides a demonstration on how to do impacts assessment (see www.training.sustainabilityprofessionals.org).
- SPaRK™, the *Sustainability Planning and Reporting Kit*, includes an Excel version of the high-level impacts assessment described below (see www.axisperformance.com for more information).
- *Lean and Environment Toolkit* published by the US Environmental Protection Agency shows how and where to integrate environmental factors in a process diagram (see www.epa.gov/lean/toolkit/LeanEnviroToolkit.pdf).

METHODS AND INSTRUCTIONS

In this chapter we offer three ways of conducting an impact assessment (see Table 4.1).

High-level impact assessment

When to use. This high-level approach is a good way to quickly understand your organization's major impact areas and to begin to see what pursuing sustainability would mean to your organization.

How to prepare. Convene a cross-representational group from your organization so that all the critical functions are represented. Make sure that the members of this group have

Table 4.1 *Overview of methods for identifying priorities*

Process	When to use
High-level impact assessment	This simple approach to conducting an impact analysis is quick and easy, while still resulting in the critical information that you need to launch a sustainability effort. This can also be a useful precursor to the aspects and impact process below.
Aspect- and impact-weighted criteria assessment	This approach is useful when you want a more detailed approach to your impact analysis and when you are considering a large number of impacts. It will likely appeal to organizations with an environmental management system. Unlike the version above, it provides quantifiable results.
Process mapping	The process mapping approach is appropriate if you are focusing on your core processes and want to find efficiencies in addition to impacts.

a good understanding of sustainability and are familiar with the framework or guiding principles that you have chosen for your organization.

How to conduct this activity. Display or photocopy handouts of Figure 4.1 and explain what is implied or included in each of the 'bubbles':

- *Energy* includes all of the power (electricity, natural gas, propane, etc.) needed to run your operation, as well as the fuel used to transport people and products.
- *Materials* are all the inputs and products that go into your products and are consumed by your administrative functions.
- *Processes* refer to the major activities that occur within your organization. If you are a manufacturing organization, then certainly this includes your production processes. If you are a service organization, then at the very least this would likely include meetings, document creation, customer interactions and the like.
- *Facilities* refer to your physical plant or the buildings that you occupy.
- *Employees* are meant to include the work environment and your key human resources policies.
- *Waste* is all the 'non-product' that leaves your facility.
- *Product or service* is obviously what you deliver to your customers, along with any unintended side effects.
- *Community* refers to the relationship that you have with the community (local and or global) within which you operate.
- *Industry* is meant to address your involvement and influence over your industry.

INDUSTRY

What are our strategic partners/supply chain relationships?

What would our criteria be for choosing strategic partners?

Does this give us ideas for possible projects, new relationships, things we need our industry to do for us to be successful?

Relationships with major stakeholders

PROCESSES

What are our major processes?

What would our criteria be for a sustainable process?

Does this give us ideas for possible projects?

Relationships with your community

PRODUCTS & SERVICES

What are our major products and services and are there any unintended impacts associated with them?

What would our criteria be for a sustainable product/service?

Does this give us ideas for possible projects?

Major outputs →

RESIDUAL PRODUCTS/'WASTE'

What are our major residual products/waste streams?

What would our criteria be for a sustainable waste stream?

Does this give us ideas for possible projects?

COMMUNITY

What are the major challenges for our community?

What would our criteria be for choosing community issues to work on?

Does this give us ideas for possible projects?

ENERGY

What are our major sources of energy (buildings, process and transportation)?

What would our criteria be for sustainable energy?

Does this give us ideas for possible projects?

Major inputs ↑

MATERIALS

What are our major material inputs?

What would our criteria be for sustainable materials?

Does this give us ideas for possible projects?

Figure 4.1 *Impact assessment diagram*

Using Figure 4.1, lead your group through a discussion revolving around the following three questions, making notes on the diagram. We usually begin with the *processes* block in the middle of the diagram, then work on the *inputs*, the *outputs* and, last, *relationships*. Note that sometimes it can be easier to swap the order of step 1 and step 2, especially for groups who are more literal and get bogged down in abstract discussions:

1   *Criteria*: what would a sustainable version of each area of the impact assessment diagram look like? What criteria would we use to define sustainability for this aspect? (This is a good place to make use of your chosen framework or guiding principles.)
2   *Specific examples*: what currently happens in each of these areas? Where do we meet our sustainability criteria and where do we not?
3   *Ideas*: what project ideas begin to emerge from this analysis? Where are our high-impact areas? Where would it make sense to begin our journey towards sustainability?

How to debrief. Summarize your findings as a set of priorities to work on. What are your largest impacts? What are the most fruitful near-term projects? In a later meeting, use the results of the impacts assessment to build metrics and a long-term plan.

Aspect- and impact-weighted criteria assessment

When to use. This approach takes a more detailed look at your operation and involves the use of a weighted criteria chart that both identifies your impacts and helps you to simultaneously prioritize them. The time required to do this process varies significantly. You may be able to do a cursory analysis in an hour; a more rigorous approach will probably take two to three hours. This approach may be preferred by those with formal environmental management systems.

How to prepare. Before you convene the people who will participate in this process, determine the scope of your analysis. If you have multiple sites, will you take all of them into consideration or just a target few? How far upstream will you examine in terms of the materials that you use? What about end-of-life considerations for your products and services? Will you take into account the behaviours, priorities or positions of your key stakeholders, such as your customers or board of directors?

In addition, clarify the criteria you will use to assess your aspect and activities. When you assign ratings, it can be useful to have a worksheet such as in Table 4.2 that defines what each rating means. What does a 1 mean? What does a 5 mean? You can customize Table 4.2 to meet your needs. The columns should match the criteria that you are using in your impact assessment.

Table 4.2 *Sample scoring worksheet (based on The Natural Step)*

Points	System condition 1 Extraction	System condition 2 Persistence	Toxicity	System condition 3 Biodiversity	System condition 4 Efficiency and equity	Frequency	Influence
1	100% recycled	Biodegrades in less than one day	Non-toxic	Sustainably harvested Ecosystem sympathetic	Locally sourced Small percentage to landfill Energy efficient	Rarely used	Little influence
2							
3	Mixed	Biodegrades in less than one month	Moderately toxic	Mixed	Mixed	Occasional use	Some influence
4							
5	Mined	Biodegrades in more than one year	Acutely toxic	Consumes nature	Distance source High percentage to landfill Consumes a substantial amount of energy	Continuous use	Substantial influence

Source: adapted from Duke Castle (2001).

This six-item scoring system for prioritizing projects is based on the four Natural Step system conditions, as well as two additional considerations: frequency with which a product or process is used and the amount of influence that an organization feels it is able to exert in order to change it. Note that in this particular model, system condition 2 is divided into two criteria: persistence and toxicity. This, in effect, over-weights the system condition, so you may prefer to combine them. You should also discuss whether to add The Natural Step criteria and frequency/influence scores or to multiply them. As you can tell, there are implications for all these options and there is no universal right answer.

How to conduct this activity. Once you are clear on your criteria, generate a list of your organization's key activities and/or aspects. You can pull these from the high-level impact assessment diagram (see Figure 4.1), a process flow chart or, in simple operations, you can brainstorm them from scratch. You will need to determine the level of detail that you want to take with this analysis. Your list might be limited to the key activities of the organization and their biggest inputs, or you can drill down into each activity to identify the detailed aspects and sub-steps. If you are doing an impact assessment for the first time, it is probably sufficient to stay at a high level.

Create a matrix using your two lists: the list of your aspects and activities, and the list of your criteria. Enter the aspects and activities down the first column and the criteria in the fields across the first row. To give nuance to your analysis, consider whether all of the criteria you have chosen are of equal importance. If there are some that seem more important to you than others (either because of their impact or because of special relevance to your industry), assign a higher weight to them. For most organizations, we recommend keeping the rating system simple, using a scale of 1 to 3 (equivalent to a low/medium/high scale), with 3 being the most important or largest impact.

Now you are ready to conduct your analysis. For each aspect or activity listed in the first column, rate it based on how serious an impact it has – for example, a scale of 1 to 3 or a scale of 1 to 5, as in Table 4.2's scoring worksheet. If the aspect or activity is in extreme violation of the criterion, give it the highest number. If it doesn't violate it at all, give it a 1 or 0. Then multiply each rating by the weight for that criterion to obtain a score for entry into the cells in your matrix. You can then calculate a total score for each aspect to quickly arrive at high-priority issues. The example in Table 4.3 is a sample, abbreviated. It uses criteria derived from The Natural Step system conditions.

Table 4.3 *Weighted criteria matrix*

Criteria	Carbon neutral	Non-toxic	Locally sourced (within 200 miles/320km)	Zero waste	Fair labour practices	Total score
Weight	3	2	1	2	2	
Aspect or Activity						
Source ingredients for pizza	2	1	2	1	3	18
Cook pizza	3	1	1	1	1	16
Deliver pizza	3	3	1	2	1	22

Based on the hypothetical example above, the biggest impact is not in creating the pizza, but in its delivery. This would then suggest working to reduce the impacts associated with transportation through fuel-efficient vehicles, alternative fuels or improved logistics.

How to debrief. Review the biggest impacts, those with the highest total scores, emphasizing that it is tentative until the assumptions are verified. Identify any data that need to be gathered or assumptions verified, and assign responsibility for following up. The next step will be to come up with ways of measuring and reducing these impacts.

Process mapping

When to use. This approach examines your key processes. If you already have a detailed process map created from an earlier project (e.g. a value stream map for lean manufacturing), you can get double duty from that work by using this approach. This approach is most appropriate for those organizations where it is clear that one or two processes have the biggest impact. It may also be helpful for particularly complex processes with many different steps, as is often the case in manufacturing. It is also useful for identifying process waste and inefficiency that, in addition to revealing ways of reducing your environmental and social footprint, also create opportunity for productivity gains. Manufacturing, for example, may want to initially ignore its support functions, such as administration and marketing, in order to focus on its primary manufacturing process.

BOX 4.1 CREATING A PROCESS MAP

If you do not already have a process map, you may choose to create one. Process mapping is a field unto its own that is beyond the scope of this book; however, in some cases, you may only need a simple process map that can be achieved by following these steps:

1   Define the beginning and end points of your process.
2   Then brainstorm steps on sticky-backed notes so that you can move them around until you get them in the right order.
3   Then go out onto the shop floor or wherever the work is done to observe the degree to which your map matches the territory. Adjust it as appropriate.

During the heyday of the Quality Revolution, a movement that transformed industry in the 1980s, we used to say that there are three versions of the same process: what you think it is, what it really is and what it should be. Process mapping is a great tool for identifying inefficiencies; therefore, creating the map may itself yield important benefits.

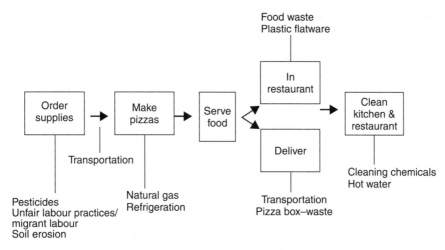

Figure 4.2 *Sample process diagram*

For an example of what this might look like, especially if you are already doing lean manufacturing, please refer to the *Lean and Environment Toolkit*, version 1, especially Figure 3 'Current state value stream map with environmental data'. The toolkit can be downloaded from www.epa.gov/lean/toolkit/LeanEnviroToolkit.pdf.

We provide a simple process diagram in Figure 4.2.

How to prepare. If you have a complicated manufacturing or work process, it is often helpful to work from a process diagram, identifying inputs and outputs for each step in the process. Check with your engineers to see if they have such a process flow diagram. Creating one from scratch is a lengthy process and is beyond the scope of this book.

How to conduct this activity:

1   Go through your process map and flag any steps that use a lot of energy, involve toxic chemicals or make heavy demands on natural resources, such as water.
2   Identify the highest priority impacts based on a set of criteria that may include urgency (regulators are breathing down your neck or costs are escalating) and feasibility (fixes are available and cost effective).

How to debrief. Review the priorities and do a gut check. Are these really the best things to focus on? Can you make a significant difference? Then build a plan to reduce the impacts that come to the top of your priority list.

Developing Sustainability Metrics and Reports

CONCEPTS AND CASE EXAMPLES

There's an old adage: what gets measured gets done. A robust set of metrics can be a powerful tool to focus attention and generate feedback. Metrics can help you to track your progress and celebrate successes.

There are, however, some important psychological dynamics that you should understand. Corporate enthusiasm for measuring performance can, in part, be linked back to behaviourism and the questionable application of that field of psychological research. Management theorists have seen metrics as either a source of feedback or, based on the behaviourists' belief that these drive behaviour, the basis of rewards. And for a hungry pigeon or rat in a cage, this is certainly true. If they have to press a bar to get a food pellet, they will quickly learn to do so.

However, humans are decidedly more complex, and no one ever asked the rat or pigeon how they felt about this arrangement. When offered the freedom of an open cage door, they are far more likely to flee than remain on the food pellet assembly line. Alfie Kohn (1986, 1993) has convincingly written about the unintended consequences of rewards on humans and they include deflecting the attention from the task to the reward and devaluing the task. If you remove the reward, people, too, will often flee the task.

Employees resent feeling manipulated by metrics and other management control systems. We once knew a manager who had worked incredibly hard to develop a gain-sharing programme (where financial benefits are shared with the employees) – not an easy task in government – only to have his engineers shout back: 'Don't insult us! We do good work because it's the right thing to do. Don't think that by dangling a carrot in front of us you will change our performance.'

For these very reasons, some people often fear and resist metrics. Be prepared to answer questions about how the metrics will be used, who will see them and how they will be gathered. Be careful not to undermine such intrinsic motivators as pride in a job well done or excitement over improving an environmental or social impact. The following guidelines should help you to navigate the common pitfalls.

Fundamental principles

Before you develop a set of metrics, consider a few fundamental principles.

Use metrics for learning, not major consequences. Use metrics as a way of learning, not of meting out rewards or punishments. If you attach significant consequences (which may be something as seemingly insignificant as an executive talking up the results), people will game the system.

Ensure a balanced set of metrics. What gets measured *does* tend to get done, sometimes at the expense of things you forgot to measure. If you focus just on greenhouse gases, you may inadvertently lead to increased natural resource depletion (e.g. rainforests being chopped down for palm oil plantations) or other unintended side effects. A focus on eliminating solid waste can lead to decisions to release the same waste to water or air. Be sure your system of metrics isn't setting you up to trade one problem for another.

Measure at the right scale. If you set metrics on too small a scale, you can set up employees to compete with one another when, in fact, you need them to cooperate. There are many systemic barriers to cooperation in organizations that stem from getting these boundaries wrong. The person managing the capital budget doesn't want to spend extra on more energy-efficient equipment because the benefits would show up in the operations budget. The information technology manager doesn't want to swap out old mainframes even though the energy savings alone would pay for it in a couple of years because it will create new work for him while the savings will show up on someone else's budget. Alternatively, you should avoid measuring at too large a scale where people don't feel like they can affect the outcome. Life-cycle costing and activity-based costing can help to allocate impacts down to a level that will make sense to employees. The proper scale is often determined by the thing you are measuring, whether or not you can control all of it. For example, outdoor air quality is largely a measure of the air shed, not just the emissions of your own building.

Let those who need the information measure what matters. Measuring and reviewing the metrics takes time, so be sure that you are measuring things that will make a difference, not frivolous things. And, wherever possible, have the people who will use the data be the ones to gather them. Otherwise, you'll spend all your time cajoling people to complete reports. You will also get a more immediate response since people who get real time feedback on performance tend to make real time adjustments and corrections.

Limit the number of metrics needing attention at any one time. People can't pay attention to 20 or 100 metrics or goals. Psychologists have shown that the human brain can hold approximately seven items simultaneously. So, narrowing down the metrics that any one person has to look at to a handful is a good idea. This may seem to violate the principle of having a full set of metrics; but there are ways around this problem:

- *Nesting/indices.* If you nest metrics so that they roll up to an index, you can track the index and only tunnel down into the sub-measures if needed – for example, water temperature, concentration of chemicals and turbidity can all roll up to a water quality index. Some organizations are experimenting with using our SCORE™ sustainability assessment as a way of rolling up their entire sustainability performance into one number that they can compare over time.
- *Assignments.* Ask different people to keep track of different measures. Periodically meet to discuss the interactions between the measures.
- *Focus.* Pick a couple of measures to focus on for a quarter or a year, rotating through a balanced set over time. You could, for example, focus on one Natural Step system condition during each quarter.
- *Exceptions.* Only look at metrics when they fall outside of acceptable ranges. You could, for example, call attention to recycling rates when they are lower *or* higher than expected.

Combine leading and lagging metrics. Lagging metrics measure things in the past and leading metrics help you to predict the future. Energy use is a lagging metric; but investment in energy conservation is a leading indicator. Crime statistics are a lagging indicator, while teen pregnancies and the percentage of young unemployed men are leading indicators.

Define ongoing and project-specific metrics. Some of your metrics should be tracked over the long term so that you can compare results year after year. Others may only be tracked for a short period to assess the effectiveness of an initiative. Many organizations, for example, should track greenhouse gas emissions year after year. At AXIS, however, we have offset all of our identifiable greenhouse gas emissions for close to a decade, so that would make a very boring chart! Instead, we calculate our greenhouse gas emissions for the purpose of offsetting them, but we report on the percentage of trips we take using alternative transportation. Often, shorter-term metrics are tied to specific projects. For example, if you have a paper reduction goal for the year, you'll want to report against your baseline; but you may not have a paper-use chart in every year's sustainability report.

Draft your sustainability report before gathering data. It will save you a lot of wasted time if you mock up your sustainability report before you begin gathering data. Figure out what charts you'll want to include, including the chart type and legend. Do you just want to show solid waste or do you want stacked bars showing the different types of waste in the waste stream? Figuring this out now will ensure that the data you do gather can actually produce the information you want.

Review the Global Reporting Initiative (GRI). Large publicly traded corporations should consider following the GRI. While the total number of corporations using this standard is still small, we expect it to grow. The GRI is so detailed that it goes beyond the scope of what we can cover in this book (see www.globalreporting.org).

Consider other reporting protocols. There are other reporting protocols that are being created that should be followed if you plan to make public claims. The Greenhouse Gas Protocol is an accepted standard for reporting climate impacts. The US federal government is currently updating guidelines for green marketing. If you plan to compare yourself or your products to those of competitors, or if you expect investors to be making financial decisions, in part, based on your sustainability report, a higher degree of rigor and transparency will be needed.

Make them memorable. After a few zeros, numbers cease to be meaningful to most people. They know 1 trillion is more than 1 billion is more than 1 million. But the brain just registers 'big number'. To make matters worse, many units of measurement are foreign to people. How big is a megawatt or a therm? What exactly is a metric tonne of CO_2? To make people *care* about the numbers, you have to present them in ways that are meaningful in every day life. We often convert the greenhouse gas numbers into an estimate of forestland that they would have to maintain. In Portland, Oregon, Forest Park is a well-loved feature in our community of close to 5000 acres (2020ha), so when we tell clients

---

BOX 5.1 MAKING METRICS MEMORABLE AT SCHWABE, WILLIAMSON AND WYATT

Schwabe, Williamson and Wyatt, a large attorney firm in Portland, Oregon, requested a sustainability assessment. Paper was, not surprisingly, expected to be a major impact. We queried their director of operations to find out how much paper they consumed in the previous year. But we didn't just report the number in dollars or cases. To make it more visual, we imagined the reams stacked one upon the other, and reported how many times the height of their skyscraper their paper use represented. To make it personal, we also reported the usage per attorney: how many stories high the stack of paper was that each attorney used.

When we reported these results, there was a hoot and a snort in the audience. The metrics were so startling that it galvanized their efforts to implement serious paper reduction efforts. In the first year, they switched to recycled content letterhead and reduced their reams per attorney by 6 per cent, even though their workload increased. These changes alone represented an estimated saving of US$20,000 per year. They continue to work on developing an electronic document system, a project that was started before their sustainability initiative, which should radically reduce their paper use further while improving productivity.

how many Forest Parks they'd have to buy, plant and maintain, they have a way of visualizing their greenhouse gas emissions.

Should targets be realistic or audacious?

There are two schools of thought about setting targets. The first is that goals or targets should be realistic and based on what is possible. For example, by upgrading lighting and improving insulation, we should expect to get X per cent improvement, so that is our goal. The advantage of this approach is that it is often easier for people to support because they can envision the steps necessary to accomplish it. The downside is that it only usually achieves incremental improvements.

To reach full sustainability, though, a quantum leap in performance is necessary, so some long-term radical stretch goals are needed. If you choose 'zero waste' as a goal for example, this will often generate more radical innovations than if you just strive for a 5 per cent reduction in waste every year. You often can't get there just with incremental improvements. You have to rethink the design of the product or call into question your existing business model.

Radical stretch goals can lead to employee cynicism if the goals are not based on an external standard (e.g. the requirements of nature or the performance of the industry leader). But when presented well, radical stretch goals will often produce more significant improvements.

So think about your situation. Chances are, you'll need some of both. With an existing facility or manufacturing process, you'll probably mostly strive for incremental improvements. But whenever you design a new building or product or spend significant capital, this is the best time to set radical stretch goals.

Linking your metrics to your framework

Your sustainability framework(s) should influence your choice and organization of your metrics, as well as the type of work you do. Tables 5.1 and 5.2 list recommended metrics associated with two of the more common frameworks: The Natural Step and triple bottom line.

We often nest The Natural Step system conditions (system conditions 1 to 4) into the triple bottom line. We also like to distinguish between internal and external metrics. If you don't do this, the 'economy' often becomes simply an internal profitability measure, a poor cousin to its larger purpose.

In our *Sustainability Planning and Reporting Kit*, we link metrics to each part of our impact assessment (see 'High-level impact assessment' in Chapter 4). We then provide spreadsheets to calculate each of these metrics.

Table 5.1 *Common metrics tied to The Natural Step framework*

System condition	Possible metrics
1 Substances from the Earth's crust	Greenhouse gases: metric tonnes of CO_2 equivalent (will necessarily include energy use by type); may be measured over a baseline such as Kyoto Protocol Metals: recycling rate and also recycled content
2 Human-made substances	Persistent bio-accumulative toxins: volume used Cleaning products: percentage of green cleaning products
3 Productivity of nature	Natural resources: percentage from a certified sustainable source (including paper and other wood products, agricultural products, fish, etc.) Water: conservation measured by reduction of use over baseline
4 Human needs	Employee satisfaction: measured by annual or biannual survey International labour standards: measured against SA 8000 or social audits

Table 5.2 *Common metrics tied to the triple bottom line*

	Environmental	Social (system condition 4)	Economic
Internal	Energy conservation (system condition 1) Green cleaning products (system condition 2) Water conservation (system condition 3) Green purchasing (system condition 3)	Employee satisfaction Employee retention	Profitability Living wage
External	Greenhouse gases (system condition 1) Toxic emissions (system condition 2)	Labour practices of suppliers Customer satisfaction Charity (hours and dollars)	Sales of green/certified products (system conditions 1 to 4) Local purchases Investments in sustainable businesses

Table 5.3 *Common metrics tied to impact assessment*

Area	Metrics
Energy/climate	Greenhouse gases – climate neutral
	Energy efficiency – greenhouse gas (GHG)/$
Materials	Percentage of purchases from sustainable source
Major processes	Percentage of employees paid living wage and benefits
	New buildings/remodels qualifying for Leadership in Energy and Environmental Design (LEED) Silver or better as a function of existing buildings (EB) points and/or floor space
Products/services	Percentage of sales from sustainable/green products/services
'Residual products'/waste	Percentage solid waste diverted from landfill
	Recycling rate as a percentage of total waste
Strategic partners/ supply chain	Percentage of major suppliers who have sustainability efforts under way
Community	Profits and time donated
	Local sourcing as a percentage of total purchases

BOX 5.2 SELLEN CONSTRUCTION: MEASURING GREEN BUILDING PROJECTS AS A CORE COMPETENCY

In addition to measuring your internal impacts, you will also want to measure the sustainability of your core products and services: your mission-related impacts. Sellen Construction based in Seattle, Washington, is measuring their progress towards building more sustainable projects by tracking and forecasting their clients' pursuit of Leadership in Energy and Environmental Design (LEED) projects. Yancy Wright, sustainable initiatives manager, said:

> Many of our clients have recently adopted LEED Silver and in some cases Gold as their standard project expectation. Tracking this trend is critical for understanding the level of preparedness required to meet this surge in green building requests. In 2005, only 7 per cent of our annual volume accounted for projects aiming for LEED certification. In 2007, it was up to 18 per cent and by 2010, we expect 91 per cent of our annual volume to be projects in pursuit of LEED certification.

A shortlist of critical metrics

After a while, you'll see similar metrics show up repeatedly. This is our shortlist of metrics, heavily influenced by The Natural Step. You probably should have a good excuse if these goals and metrics aren't part of your suite:

- *Climate neutral.* Show greenhouse gases at least for your own operations. You may choose to also include impacts associated with employee commuting, embodied energy in major purchases, and the customer use and disposal of your product.
- *Zero toxics.* Often the simplest way is to show volume of persistent bio-accumulative toxins purchased or in use. If you don't use any, then you can show the percentage of green cleaning products or landscaping products.
- *Zero waste.* Measure waste diverted from landfill and total waste (including recycling).
- *Sustainable natural resources.* If you use significant quantities of natural resources (e.g. water, wood products, fish and agricultural produce), show the percentage coming from sustainable sources.
- *Social impact – internal.* Have some measure of the quality of work life. Depending upon your situation, this may be the percentage of employees paid a living wage, the ratio of highest to lowest paid worker, average wages by gender or race, employee satisfaction survey results, etc.
- *Social impact – external.* Depending upon the nature of your business, this may include metrics related to international labour practices (e.g. SA 8000 results), local purchasing, and/or charitable endeavours (time and money donated).

Data traps to avoid

As you develop a list of potential metrics and begin to gather data on them, do a test run. This is especially important if more than one person is involved in collecting the data. The devil is always in the detail. Imagine you run a pizza restaurant. Here are some of the problems you may encounter:

- *Timeframes don't line up.* Your electricity bill shows usage through the 20th of the month. The natural gas bill shows the 10th of the month. You do your accounting based on a calendar month that includes production data about the number of pizzas produced. How are you going to show energy use per pizza under these circumstances?
- *People log data differently.* Your electricity bill for December arrives in January and is paid in February. In which month should its usage be logged?
- *Data are segmented differently.* You plan to report on waste by category, and you've agreed on the different categories of waste: food, plastics, liquid, etc. As different

people sort through the trash, what do they do with the plastic packets of red peppers in oil? Is it plastic, food waste or liquid?

See how important it can be to test your data-gathering methods before you deploy them? Be sure to document your decisions, train others in them and audit them periodically. Otherwise, you'll not be able to trust the figures.

Narrow down your list of metrics

Once you have a potential list of metrics, you will probably still have too many to track and report. Use the following criteria to help you winnow them down to a reasonable scoreboard:

- *Availability.* There are many measures that your organization may already track which, with a little work, can translate into useful metrics. For example, in manufacturing, engineers often have percentage efficiency numbers for each manufacturing line that can be converted to waste stream numbers. You may have trouble getting historical baseline data because you never tracked the indicator before. In some cases, you may need to use surrogates – for example, you might prefer to track the weight of items, but your computer database only tracks dollars. Our advice is to shoot for indicators that will give you evidence of progress, not necessarily scientific proof. Start with what you have and work to improve the system over time.
- *Relevance.* A metric answers a question; but your stakeholders will have different questions. Engineers and scientists, for example, may want technical details on water quality; but your customers and community may be primarily interested in the effects on salmon runs. Think about the audiences for your metrics and try to find metrics that can be reported in different ways to meet these different needs.
- *Proxies.* Sometimes one metric can be used as a proxy for others. For example, in the Pacific Northwest, salmon are often used as an indicator of overall ecosystem health, not only of the riparian area, but also of entire watersheds. They are highly symbolic for Native Americans and more recent arrivals. If the salmon appear to be in trouble – as they are – you then have to drill down to understand why. Is the decline due to water quality or quantity or temperature? Is it overharvesting or effects of hatchery-raised fish? Are forestry practices or road run-off polluting the streams?

Tips on designing graphs

Use normative and *absolute numbers.* Many numbers are only relevant in comparison with other numbers – for example, solid waste per unit of production. If the volume of solid waste is going down, you don't know whether this is because you are more efficient or because you shut down a production line since sales were soft. So many of your metrics should be a ratio, with the denominator being units of production, number of employees, sales revenue, market share, etc. This is often referred to as 'normalizing your data.'

At the same time, normative data can leave you feeling good when, from the Earth's perspective, things are still getting worse. While cars pollute much less than a decade ago, the overall pollution from cars continues to rise because there are so many more automobiles on the road now. So we encourage you to track both normative numbers and absolute numbers. Often you can show both on the same graph, using two different scales (see Figure 5.1).

Pick the best type of graph. There are many different types of graphs and each tends to highlight certain relationships and obscure others. Pie charts show the relative parts to a whole; but they don't show whether the pie is getting bigger or smaller. Bar graphs depict change over time. Stacked bar graphs are a compromise between a bar graph and a pie chart, showing some of both. Control charts show how performance compares to acceptable limits over time. Spider diagrams (also known as polar diagrams) can demonstrate many metrics at one time. Pick the graph that most accurately shows what you need to know.

Show more than one metric on a chart. One way of showing interrelationships between metrics is to graph more than one metric on the same chart. You can show more than one

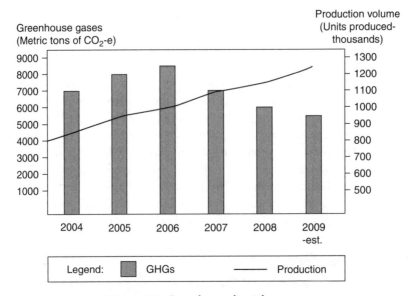

Figure 5.1 *Sample graph with two axes*

scale on the vertical axis by using one scale on the left and another on the right. In this way, you can depict, for example, both recycling rates per unit of sales and total recycling volume. Usually the horizontal axis represents time.

Make the direction of your graphs consistent. If you post a bunch of line graphs or bar charts, it can be very helpful if you design the metrics so that up (or down) is always good. This will mean that you may have to measure quality instead of defects, materials efficiency instead of waste, employee retention instead of turnover. In some cases, this requires some verbal gymnastics (e.g. percentage to carbon neutrality). But at a glance, you'll be able to see which metrics have a negative trend.

Annotate interventions. Write notes on the charts about changes that you made to the process so that it's easier to see the impact your actions have had. For example, show when you installed a new motor, replaced a chemical, instituted a recycling programme, started sales of a new product, or conducted a green marketing campaign. Don't make everyone figure it out for themselves.

Have the title tell the story. Consider modifying the titles of your graphs so that the meaning is clear. Instead of just 'energy use', why not change the title each month? 'Energy: New motors cut electricity by 500 kilowatt hours per month' is much more informative. This is particularly important to do when you use graphs in presentations because people may not have time to examine the graph in detail.

RESOURCES

General tools for reporting and metrics:

- The Global Reporting Initiative provides an international standard for sustainability reporting and is most appropriate for large publicly traded companies. However, their list of core indicators is a useful touchstone for choosing any organization's metrics. If you are going to measure something covered in their guidelines, you may as well measure it the same way in case, at some point, you need to be compliant with GRI (see www.global reporting.org).
- The World Business Council on Sustainable Development has sustainable development reporting guidelines and other resources (see www.wbcsd.org).
- The Corporate Register (see www.corporateregister.com) lists non-financial reports, including sustainability and corporate social responsibility reports from public companies all over the world. It also has awards for the best ones in different categories. See its *Global Winners and Reporting Trends* report for the most recent year. Use this resource to see what others are doing. It can be a good warm-up exercise to have all of your participants review at least one sustainability report and bring notes about what they liked and didn't like. This analysis can provide guidelines for your own report.

- The *Guide to Sustainable Community Indicators* by Maureen Hart provides a number of useful examples and resources for community-based metrics (see www.sustainable measures.com).
- SPaRK™ is the *Sustainability Planning and Reporting Kit* developed by AXIS that includes an MS Excel file of common metrics linked to an MS Word template for a sustainability plan and internal report such that charts and graphs are pulled into the right places. This tool, or at least the outline of the sections of the report template, may be helpful as you design your report (see www.axisperformance.com for more information).
- GEMI SD Planner is an interactive webtool (see www.gemi.org/docs/PubTools.htm).

Greenhouse gas tools:

- See the Greenhouse Gas Protocol for an international standard for reporting greenhouse gases (www.ghgprotocol.org).
- The World Resources Institute helped to create a number of free calculators that you can download, including ones for such common sources as commuting and facilities. They also have calculators for carbon-intensive sectors such as aluminium and cement production (see www.ghgprotocol.org/calculation-tools).
- For a concise booklet on reducing office climate impacts, see www.wri.org/publication/working-9-5-climate-change-office-guide.
- The US Environmental Protection Agency has a calculator for greenhouse gases (see www.epa.gov/cleanenergy/energy-resources/calculator.html).
- The US Environmental Protection Agency also has a web-based calculator that converts greenhouse gas emissions into everyday metrics (see www.epa.gov/cleanenergy/energy-resources/calculator.html). For example, it can convert into these units:

  - driving a particular number of cars for a year;
  - using a particular amount of gasoline or barrels of oil;
  - using a particular number of tanker trucks' worth of gasoline;
  - providing energy to a particular number of homes for a year;
  - growing trees across a particular number of acres for a year.

- The Climate Trust has calculators for businesses, events, employee commuting and citizens (see www.carboncounter.org).
- Calculators for air miles include Webflyer (see www.webflyer.com/travel/milemarker/) and Terrapass (see www.terrapass.com/flight/).
- If you want to understand carbon offsets/credits, read *Voluntary Carbon Markets* (Bayon et al, 2007).

Solid waste resources:

- The California Integrated Waste Management Board provides conversion factors for volume and weight by material type (see www.ciwmb.ca.gov/LgLibrary/DSG/ApndxI.htm).

Paper calculators and tools:

- Environmental Defense offers a paper calculator (see www.papercalculator.org/).
- The Environmental Paper Assessment Tool (www.epat.org) is more of a purchasing tool but would give you detailed information about various impacts associated with your paper purchases, down to the mill level.

Toxics:

- Measuring the level of toxins in your process is a complicated endeavour. If you can't find easy alternatives right off the bat (e.g. by specifying green cleaning products and landscape practices), you will likely have to complete a chemical inventory. Resources for this that we're aware of include the following:
  - Dolphin Software has Green Product Selector, which helps you to identify safer chemicals for particular purposes (www.dolphinsafesource.com).
- McDonough Braungart Design Chemistry (MBDC) is a consultancy focused on helping clients to implement cradle-to-cradle design (see www.mbdc.com/).

METHODS AND INSTRUCTIONS

Table 5.4 lists the tools related to metrics and reporting that are the focus of this section.

Table 5.4 *Overview of methods for metrics and reporting*

Process	When to use
Sustainability scorecard	When you need to figure out what metrics you will measure.
Metrics worksheet	When you know which metrics you plan to track.
Sustainability report template	When you need to decide what to include in a sustainability plan and how to organize it.

Sustainability scorecard

When to use. Use this process to develop a system for gathering and reporting sustainability metrics.

How to prepare. Post flip charts around the room with each element of your sustainability framework (e.g. The Natural Step system condition or social/economic/environmental). Print out possible metrics from any source you think relevant. You might, for example, print out the core indicators from the Global Reporting Initiative, metrics you already report, or metrics from other companies' sustainability reports. You may also want to bring a listing of your major impacts, sustainability assessment results or sustainability goals. Also bring post-its and a marker.

How to conduct this activity:

1   Give each person some of the sample metrics that you gathered. Have each person look at the ones they have been provided and decide which, if any, might be good for the organization to track and report. Have them place those on the appropriate flip chart. If desired, assign different people varying stakeholders (management, customers, certain NGOs, investors, etc.). If you don't have sample metrics, you can ask them to brainstorm metrics that they would hope to see in a sustainability report using post-it notes.
2   Review the flip charts as a group. Eliminate duplicates. Nest metrics (e.g. electricity usage is nested under greenhouse gas emissions) by stacking them above or below one another. If you have glaring holes, fill them.
3   Analyse the list and try to categorize them. Chances are, you'll have too many metrics. Which ones are important to measure now? Which should you likely report on every year? Which are either too hard to gather or not worth the effort?

Metrics worksheet

When to use. Use this process to develop a system for gathering and reporting sustainability metrics.

How to prepare. Create a chart similar to the worksheet below.

How to conduct this activity. Take the metrics that made the cut from the previous exercise and assign clusters of metrics to small groups in order to complete the metrics worksheet. It can be helpful to do one metrics worksheet as a whole group so that everyone can understand the process. You can do this by framework element, impact area or metric:

1   Name the metric area (framework element, impact area or metric cluster).
2   Describe the fully sustainable state under ultimate goal. If you have it, also give the baseline.

3 Identify where you can get the data.
4 Identify how you will want the data segmented under 'What to track separately' (see Table 5.5). For example, if your area is waste, do you want to segment the data by food waste, paper, construction debris, etc?
5 Under 'How to compute' (see Table 5.5), indicate any calculations or sources of factors.
6 Draw a sample chart that clearly shows the elements that the charts should contain. Is it a pie chart or a stacked bar chart? Do you want to show sales data on the same chart with energy use to put the numbers into context?
7 Complete the 'Responsibility and frequency' (see Table 5.5) portion of the chart, indicating the tasks that must be completed to gather and report on the metric.
8 Under 'Action items' (see Table 5.5), list any other tasks that must be done to be able to gather and report data. For example, someone may need to research greenhouse gas conversion factors. Perhaps someone needs to create a spreadsheet or work with accounting to add a field to the time sheet related to air travel.

Sustainability report template

When to use. As we indicated earlier, it's helpful to mock up your sustainability report long before you plan to write one. This will give you a sense of what you want to include in the report and will define the metrics you will need to track. You can then use this document to store notes about accomplishments, testimonials and goals as the year progresses so that at the end of the year, you merely need to clean it up, incorporate the actual data and compute year-end statistics.

How to prepare. Before designing your own sustainability report, it is helpful to review a number of others. We often have students bring in samples of reports, suggesting that they choose a company they know either because they like them or dislike them; perhaps they buy their products; perhaps they work for them; maybe they revile them. In groups, students talk about what they liked and didn't like. We recommend doing the same exercise in your organization. Go to www.corporateregister.com for a list of companies that produce non-financial reports.

How to conduct this activity. The following steps are best done with a group of people. You may need to include some executives, the public relations staff, someone from accounting or information technology if they automate the data collection, and the sustainability director. Alternatively, the sustainability steering committee may use this process to recommend a structure for the report:

1 Decide on the audience or audiences for your sustainability report.
2 Determine the media that you plan to use (web, print, etc.).

Table 5.5 *Metrics worksheet (area: greenhouse gases and energy use)*

How to obtain the data:

Metric	Ultimate goal	Baseline	Sources of data	What to track separately	How to compute	Sample chart
Percentage reduction of GHG from baseline	80% reduction by 2050	Zero (10 million tonnes a year in 2008)	Electricity bills Fleet records Expense reports (airline miles and personal auto)	Electricity Natural gas Auto Airline Commuting	Use Climate Trust factors to obtain CO_2 equivalent	Percent reduction of GHGs over baseline Years
Greenhouse gases by source				Building energy Process energy Transportation		Greenhouse gases by source 6% 63% 31% Building Process Transport

Responsibility and frequency:

Who	What	When
Facility manager	Enters electricity and natural gas usage numbers into spreadsheet	Monthly, when bills arrive
Human resources manager	Conducts and compiles commuting survey	Annually, in January
Clerical team	Tracks and reports on air miles of everyone in their respective departments, entering data in the spreadsheet	Monthly, after timesheets are submitted
Board of directors	Decides on the amount of carbon offsets we can afford or need to purchase	Annually, in February
Sustainability director	Compiles data and produces report	Annually, in February Finalize metrics in March after board decision on offsets

Action items:

What	Who	When	Notes
Add employee commuting question to annual employee survey, asking round trip miles/kilometres and average number of trips per week	Human resources	Before next survey	

3   Based on your answers to questions 1 and 2, determine the parameters for your report. At a minimum, you'll want to decide the maximum number of pages/screens. It's also helpful to think through the general format. For example, if you want something to be on the web as well as in print, you may want to create a PDF document. Consider limitations. If you want something to be viewed on the screen, you'll need to avoid newsprint-style columns. Will you be able to use colour or will the document need to be printed in black and white? These will all affect what you can include in your report. You may need to set different parameters for each audience; but seek ways to serve multiple masters with the same information. Perhaps, for example, the public four-page document also serves as the executive summary for your internal sustainability report to management.

4   Use post-it notes to brainstorm different ideas or themes that you want to include. Use squiggles to indicate text that will need to be written, but write the headers. Carefully mock up the graphs and charts, specifying the type of graph, legend, timeframes, etc. Include metrics that you want to monitor year after year. Highlight important initiatives. Often there is a letter from the president at the front. If you need the report to be audited, leave room for that as well.

5   Use blank copy paper or flip chart paper to represent the different pages or screens. Organize the post-it notes onto the pages, reorganizing as needed. If applicable, use colours or symbols to indicate which elements can also be used in other settings. For example, the written sustainability report might be your most complete version; but the website could highlight a handful of key elements.

   Debrief. After you have a mock-up of the sustainability report, critique it from different points of view. You can pass it by different stakeholders for their reactions. Are we providing the type of information you want to see? Is it easy to find? You can also simulate this by assigning each person in the meeting with a different role and have them look at the mock-up from this point of view. After the meeting, create a template for the report.

6

Developing an Implementation Strategy and Choosing Projects

Concepts and case examples

In Chapter 3, you developed a long-term vision and defined the end points. Now you must figure out how to get there in a timely fashion. There are several key decisions your organization will need to make in order to approach your efforts coherently. We've broken this chapter into three key steps:

1 developing a long-term plan to reach sustainability;
2 making decisions regarding where and how to start;
3 developing a system for prioritizing and choosing projects.

Make sure to refer back to Chapter 1, especially with regard to deciding where to begin your sustainability efforts and whom to involve.

Developing a long-term plan to reach sustainability

Some things can be done right away and others may be impossible in the near future because the technology doesn't exist or other enabling factors are not yet in place. You may need to start with actions that are most likely to save you money so that you have a fund to invest in future improvements as they become more costly or difficult.

You have to plan for two types of actions:

1 how to manage the sustainability effort (process or management system);
2 what to do to improve your sustainability performance (projects).

We will cover some of the process steps in more detail in other chapters; but let us give you a thumbnail of what is involved now because you may want to include elements of these tasks in your plan.

Although every organization is unique, we have found that the following ten-step process applies in many situations:

 1 Form a steering committee.
 2 Educate yourselves about sustainability and frameworks.
 3 Examine the strategic business case for pursuing sustainability.
 4 Develop a plan with impacts, metrics and priorities.
 5 Mock up a sustainability report (including metrics).
 6 Gather baseline data and information about options.
 7 Implement the best ideas; monitor results.
 8 Conduct a formal evaluation of results and institutionalize lessons learned.
 9 Report to all relevant stakeholders.
10 Deepen your understanding.

Be sure to incorporate these steps within your implementation plan as appropriate.

In order to plan what you're going to work on, backcasting is a frequently used approach to create a comprehensive long-term plan. It forces you to keep your future vision in mind while you decide what to do in both the short and long term. Whatever planning process you use, you will want to lay out a schedule of activities that detail the major tasks, milestones and responsibilities that will ensure you achieve your vision.

Most planning processes follow these three steps:

1   Define the fully sustainable state (see Chapters 3 and 5) and estimate when you should be able to reach that state. Some goals, such as being climate neutral, are technically possible (through a combination of energy conservation, green power and carbon offsets) to do now, although you may want to ease into it over time. Other goals are technically not feasible now, but you may have reason to believe that new technologies or economic forces will eventually make them possible.
2   Lay out goals incrementally for specific periods of time between the present and that end state. We typically use 1-, 3-, 5-, 10- and 20-year timeframes. Following the example above, you may decide that you can reduce your greenhouse gases by 10 per cent per year over your current baseline with a goal of being carbon neutral in ten years.
3   Identify the projects that will help you to reach these goals. Put most of your emphasis on identifying projects for the next few years; but see if there are some near-term projects that you should consider which will help you to reach your long-term goals.

We've laid out several options for creating such a plan at the end of the chapter.

Making decisions regarding where and how to start

In other chapters, we've identified a number of questions that you'll want to answer, including what's the business case for doing this and what framework(s) to use? There are a few more questions you'll want to address that will inform your understanding about how best to get started or what to do next:

- How does sustainability relate to what you've already done?
- Where should you start?
- And who needs to be on board?

How does sustainability relate to what you've already done? Sustainability efforts rarely emerge in a vacuum. To avoid the 'programme of the month' cynicism, it can be helpful to explicitly link your sustainability efforts to familiar programmes in the organization. Do you have an environmental management system that could be strengthened to be a sustainability management system? Is your organization a long-time advocate of total quality management, lean manufacturing or related efforts? Do you have a longstanding practice of empowering employee work teams? If so, perhaps you can show how sustainability is a logical extension of them.

Box 6.1 Symbolic actions make a splash

Many organizations start their formal sustainability efforts with a symbolic action. Ashforth Pacific, a West Coast property management and construction firm, implemented a 'cookies for trash cans' project in which employees got cookies in exchange for agreeing to give up their trash cans and throwing all of their garbage away in a central bin. This simple project was easy for employees to participate in and saved the company 9000 plastic trashcan liners a year.

Source: Oregon Natural Step Network (2002)

Developing a system for choosing projects

Sometimes the place to begin is obvious. If you are constructing a new building, adding a new production line or making other decisions with long-term ramifications, then start there. Often, though, you will have to choose from among lots of interesting ideas. In these cases we recommend establishing criteria for selecting projects. Your decision-makers should have a good deal of input to this criteria set. We often begin our work with clients by asking the leadership a set of key questions:

- What expectations do you have for the results of this effort?
- What priorities do you have either in terms of issues to address or problems to avoid? Have you been cited for violating an environmental regulation? Have your customers or shareholders been asking for social or environmental improvements?
- Are there any thresholds that projects must meet before they can be implemented?

The answers to these questions help sustainability teams or steering committees to generate ideas that are more likely to have the backing of the decision-makers. We take the answers to those groups and then ask the committees to turn them into specific criteria for selecting projects. We help them think in terms of five categories to ensure that they have a full complement of decision-making information.

Impact. Logically, the actions to consider first are those that will have the highest positive impact upon your triple bottom line (economy, environment and society). We start the list of criteria with environmental impact. Your impacts analysis, which typically precedes your project selection process, will have identified and prioritized your organization's impact. Consider also balancing your choice of projects. We recommend picking both quick wins and big wins: projects that will provide you with quick success and projects that may take more time and effort, but will have a more lasting or significant impact. When considering projects with potential for quick success, think in terms of strategies that either provide a good financial return, create a positive public image or will stoke the enthusiasm and energy of your employees.

Payback or return. Financial return is always an important consideration in business decisions. In the case of picking sustainability projects, however, sequence the choice of your projects so that paybacks are attractive enough to gain leadership support while at the same time garnering enough in savings or new earnings to fund future efforts. When considering the costs and potential return on investment from projects, be sure to examine all financial aspects, not just the obvious or immediate ones. There are at least five categories worth exploring as described in Table 6.1.

BOX 6.2 MAKING SENSE OF DATA

Dolphin Software has developed a tool to compare different chemicals (e.g., cleaning products, solvents, etc.) both in terms of their environmental characteristics on one axis and cost on the other. They graph these so it is easy to see which products have both a low environmental impact and a low cost. Similarly, Austin Energy is spearheading the creation of a system to help utilities compute a carbon return on investment, the cheapest methods for reducing the largest amount of greenhouse gases.

Table 6.1 *Cost-benefit categories*

Cost category	Definition
Direct financial benefits or costs	These are costs, savings or additional revenues that are easy to identify. These usually include material, labour, direct expenses or revenues that are usually allocated to a product or process (e.g. raw materials for production, paper costs for office activities, etc.).
Hidden savings or costs	These are expenses or revenues that are not easily allocated to products or services but are, nonetheless, related. Do you spend time fending off angry non-profits? Do your chemicals require special training and handling? Do you need lots of quality assurance steps to maintain a safe workplace?
Risk avoidance	These are costs or benefits that are derived from the occurrence of a possible future event (e.g. clean-up costs from materials spills, health costs from exposure, liability for litigation or other claims, etc.).
Image or relationship	These are costs/benefits that are associated with your organization's reputation in your community or with your customers or shareholders. These days, public corporations can derive more of their value from these intangibles than their physical plant and equipment.
Externalities	These costs and benefits may be hard to estimate but represent the impacts for which the organization does not have to account. Is someone else breathing your pollution? Are your greenhouse gas emissions contributing to climate change? What is the value of restoring a watershed? You may be able to get paid for certain ecosystem service benefits associated with greenhouse gases, flood control, water temperature, endangered species, etc.

It can be helpful to separate the sustainability benefits of your ideas from their costs and graph them.

Feasibility. Some projects will just be easier to do than others. You will need to define for your own business what is feasible and what is not. This may necessitate clarifying up front what your organization's tolerance is for possible disruption of business processes, changes in relationships with vendors or customers, or limits on capital expenditures. The sooner these criteria are identified, the more efficient your project selection process will be.

Leverage. Consider your project options from the point of view of leverage or transferability. There might be a project that you are considering that at first sight doesn't provide high return, but has potential for affecting efforts down the line. For example, let's say you use solvents in many areas of your production. If you could find a more benign solvent for cleaning parts, that same solvent might be used in the other applications as well, solving many problems at once.

Another factor to consider is long-term payback. The Natural Step framework favours what are called 'platform' strategies. A platform strategy is one that by itself may not return high value, but that enables later high-return solutions. It prepares you to take advantage of future developments and provides flexibility, not locking you into one approach. For example, an architect might design a building to maximize a south-facing roof area so that solar cells could be added later. You might wire your facility for diesel back-up generators in anticipation of installing a hydrogen fuel cell later, even though using a diesel generator might seem to be a step in the wrong direction.

Appeal and visibility. After all is said and done, some projects will just have more emotional appeal than others. Reducing your workforce commutes, for example, may not be as appealing to employees, customers or community members as something like achieving zero waste. Sometimes, how you frame the issue can make all the difference. 'Saving the salmon' may have more appeal than 'improving water quality'. Appeal is an especially important criterion if you are using your sustainability efforts to increase employee or customer loyalty. If you are trying to sell sustainability to the leaders of your organization, you may need to implement early projects that will appeal to their own passions or notions of responsible behaviour.

Managing the load

We're not aware of a commonly used term for what we want to explain, so we need to resort to a metaphor. Perhaps you have seen the vaudeville act where a performer spins plates on top of poles. He starts spinning one plate on a poll, then puts another plate on a second poll, then another and another. Soon the first dish starts to wobble and the performer rushes over and twirls the pole to get it going again. This is a useful metaphor for what we want to cover next because it emphasizes the need to pay at least a modicum of attention to all the plates in play, lest they come crashing down. The number of plates a performer can keep in the air is a function of his skill. Some are even able to spin cups and saucers, an even more ambitious task because they spin at different rates.

So the question is this: what is your capacity for change? How many sustainability dishes can you keep in the air and how many different kinds before organizational gravity flings them to the ground? Some of your plates are likely to be large, others small. Putting labels to these dishes is an important exercise.

Here are examples of some common variations:

- A city decided to have one to three priorities per year that all agencies would focus on; each agency was then expected to come up with one other sustainability goal that they would pursue on their own.

- A county assembled a team of sustainability liaisons for every department and each quarter they picked a sustainability policy or metric to work on together.
- A museum chose different projects that, among them, would, first, make a significant environmental difference; second, educate and involve employees; and, third, be visible to and educational for visitors.
- A manufacturer formed a steering committee of executives that worked through a sustainability award programme, criterion by criterion, picking one thing to focus on each month (e.g. water conservation and elimination of aerosol cans).
- An insurance company decided to pursue a big win for the year, as well as a quick win and a community-focused charitable effort each quarter.

You could also:

- Choose one issue such as climate change and have every department define what they can do to affect it.
- Focus on one 'big win' a year and have a list of 'quick wins' that you address one at a time.
- Address a different Natural Step system condition every quarter.

You get the picture. There isn't a universal right answer. The purpose is to make sure that you don't take on too many projects or miss important selection criteria (e.g. having no projects during the year that are visible to employees). We often recommend thinking in terms of big wins/quick wins, as well as having at least one project that everyone can get behind (so you can roll out impressive results and build a sense of camaraderie), while also encouraging initiatives in individual departments.

Ultimately, it's helpful to build this into a table so that it's clear whether you have the right number and types of plates. We provide a couple of examples in Tables 6.2 to 6.3.

Tips for choosing projects

- Go for quick wins and big wins.
- Choose a variety of projects that will allow everyone to find their place.
- Keep some projects under wraps until you have results to show.
- Use the savings created by some projects to fund the less financially feasible but important one.

Table 6.2 *Quick win–big win*

Project type	January–March	April–June	July–September	October–November	Next year
Big win	Redesign our primary product using design for environment methods.				Life-cycle assessment comparing our product to competitors
Quick win	Create an inventory of all the green things we've done to date.	Promote alternative commuting. Initiate a bike to work day.	Set up a 'waste not' materials exchange fair.	Conduct energy conservation audit of offices.	Possible ideas:
Community outreach	Establish a food drive.	Initiate a stream restoration project.	Hold a plastics recycling event.	Hold a toy drive.	
Employee education	Have a discussion course on sustainability concepts.	Invite a guest speaker on telecommuting.	Invite a guest speaker on green purchasing.	Invite a guest speaker on climate change.	Ideas:

RESOURCES

- Epstein, M. (2008) *Making Sustainability Work: Best Practices in Managing and Measuring Corporate Social, Environmental and Economic Impacts*, Greenleaf Publishing, Sheffield, UK
- Doppelt, B. (2003) *Leading Change toward Sustainability*, Greenleaf Publishing, Sheffield, UK

METHODS AND INSTRUCTIONS

In this section, we explain four activities or processes that are helpful in developing a business case for sustainability.

Long-term project plan

When to use. Once you have chosen a framework and sustainability metrics, you can begin laying out a plan to get to a fully sustainable state.

Table 6.3 Company-wide goal plus departmental projects

Project type	January–March	April–June	July–September	October–November	Next year
Company wide	Paper and waste reduction				Toxics reduction
Administration department	Develop a method for reporting on paper use.	Inventory all appliances/equipment to see how much qualifies for Energy Star (or similar certification).	Identify the most environmentally friendly copy paper.	Create a 'Top 10' list of the products that contain toxics.	Possible ideas:
Procurement department	Develop a green purchasing policy.	Send a letter to major vendors about our sustainability efforts and expectations.	Find an alternative to aerosol paint cans.	Create contract language for our waste hauler.	Develop a grey-and-black list of chemicals.
Facilities department	Conduct a waste audit and report results	Investigate alternatives to the largest waste stream(s).	Find recyclers for plastics.	Conduct a waste audit again and compare the results.	Ideas: use Leadership in Energy and Environmental Design (LEED) for remodelling the third floor.

Table 6.4 *Overview of methods for implementation*

Purpose	When to use
Long-term project plan	Puts projects and goals into a long-term timeline.
Opportunity finder	Identifies the best place to begin your sustainability effort where need intersects with readiness.
Stakeholder assessment	Identifies strategies for getting the right people on board and properly positioned for moving forward.
Weighted criteria chart	Compares project ideas against selection criteria.

How to prepare. Create a chart similar to the one in Table 6.5. Feel free to choose timeframes other than the ones shown below. The structure in our example chart correlates with the impact assessment we introduced in Chapter 5 and we've provided a partially completed example for a pottery retailer. Depending upon the framework you choose, the categories down the left side may also be different. For example, if you are following the Global Reporting Initiative, you would likely use their structure. You could also list your major metrics or use the triple bottom line categories (social, economic and environmental).

How to conduct this activity:

1   Define the fully sustainable state (or transfer it from your vision) and write this in the long-term goal. Remind people that it may not be possible now. Some end states may be clearly dictated by an understanding of natural laws and science (e.g. The Natural Step system conditions or greenhouse gas reductions), where others may be more up to your organization to decide.

2   Working backwards from this goal, identify the interim goals that are achievable and necessary to reach the goal. Note that you may be able to reach some end-state goals in a relatively short period of time; it might be possible, for example, to eliminate all toxic chemicals from your process. But others may take a long time to achieve.

3   Develop a set of actions or project ideas that will lead you towards your goals over time.

It may be best to go through steps 1 to 3 above for one row or criterion at a time. It may take several meetings to complete a plan for all of your critical impacts. You may choose to only build a plan for a few impacts in your first year and add in new components in future years.

How to debrief. Once you have a draft plan for each of the impacts, review the plan as a whole:

Table 6.5 *Sample Sustainability Project Plan*

	Project plan			
Area	1 Year	2–3 Year	4–5 Year	Long term
ENERGY/ CLIMATE	Goal: Get baseline data on greenhouse gas emissions	Goal: Reduce natural gas 24%	Goal: Reduce greenhouse gases by 75% from baseline	Goal: Climate neutral
	Projects: Compute greenhouse gas emissions. Conduct an energy audit.	Projects: Conduct an energy audit. Install heat recovery unit and new lights.	Projects: Install new HVAC. Buy green power. Purchase carbon offsets for anything else.	Projects: Help design a kiln that works off solar energy.
MATERIALS	Goal:	Goal:	Goal:	Goal:
	Projects:	Projects:	Projects:	Projects:
MAJOR	Goal:	Goal:	Goal:	Goal:
PROCESSES	Projects:	Projects:	Projects:	Projects:
PRODUCTS/	Goal:	Goal:	Goal:	Goal:
SERVICES	Projects:	Projects:	Projects:	Projects:
RESIDUAL	Goal:	Goal:	Goal:	Goal:
PRODUCTS/ "WASTE"	Projects:	Projects:	Projects:	Projects:
STRATEGIC	Goal:	Goal:	Goal:	Goal:
PARTNERS/ SUPPLY CHAIN	Projects:	Projects:	Projects:	Projects:
COMMUNITY	Goal:	Goal:	Goal:	Goal:
	Projects:	Projects:	Projects:	Projects:

- Do a sanity check. Have you clustered too many projects into one time period? Have you exceeded your ability to 'spin that many plates'?
- Do a sequencing check. Does it make sense to switch the order of certain projects so that the results of one can feed into another?
- Do a criteria check. Do you have, in each time period, the types of projects you wanted? For example, is there a big win and a quick win in each period? Do you have a project that will be visible and keep employees engaged?

Opportunity finder

You have to start your sustainability initiative somewhere. How you begin can have a lasting effect. It will set the tone for your entire effort. It's not just a matter of deciding logically where the biggest sustainability opportunities are. It's also a matter of assessing the readiness of different parts of the organization to engage and manage the symbolism associated with your launch. You do not want to begin by forcing sustainability on those who aren't ready to engage, even if that's where the highest impact opportunities lie. Instead, try to make sustainability the most fun, cool, exciting, honouring and inspiring thing to do in your organization! You have to find where need and readiness intersect.

To that end, we've developed what we're calling an opportunity finder (see Table 6.6). This simple table should help you to root out the best place(s) to begin your sustainability effort. The top part of the table examines needs – in other words, where the major opportunities are to make a difference. The bottom section assesses readiness.

When to use. This exercise is most useful for those trying to find their entry point for bringing sustainability into the organization as a formal initiative. It can also be used the first few times you do a sustainability plan or start one in a new division.

How to prepare. Complete a chart similar to Table 6.6, listing your departments or divisions across the top.

How to conduct this activity.

1   Examine each department against the criteria in the left column. Make notes and check marks as appropriate.
2   Analyse the chart to identify which departments or divisions might be the best place to start. Are all the parties ready to participate or are there more actions you should take to get them ready?

In Table 6.6, we've filled in the cells for a fictional organization. Notice that while *manufacturing* has most of the needs, it's not ready to engage, whereas the *design engineers* are probably the place to begin. This table will help you to choose where to begin and/or help you to identify where you should start investigating readiness.

How to debrief. Based on your assessment, decide what your entry point should be. If all relevant stakeholders don't have an X in the readiness section, decide what needs to be done to help them get ready. Build an action plan for moving forward.

Stakeholder assessment

If you have a diverse set of stakeholders, it can sometimes be helpful to analyse how supportive each stakeholder group is and where you need each to be. This stakeholder

Table 6.6 *Opportunity finder*

Need	Notes about your situation	Facilities	Field repair	Procurement	Manufacturing	Human resources	Design engineering
Do you have any major capital projects planned?	*Installing a new product line*				X		X
Are there certain sustainability issues that urgently need to be addressed (e.g. climate change, toxics, natural resources depletion and fair labour)?	*Climate change and energy costs*	X	X		X		
What are your major sustainability impacts and where do they occur, or are they controlled?	*Greenhouse gases, toxic materials*	X			X		X

Readiness	Notes about your situation	Facilities	Field repair	Procurement	Manufacturing	Human resources	Design engineering
Where is leadership coming from? Who is interested in sustainability and is well placed to make a difference, either because of positional authority or influence?	*Kim* *Sally* *Bill* *Rodrigo*					X	X
Where is there high awareness and interest in sustainability amongst employees?	*Green team*						X
Who has the capacity to take on a change effort right now?	*Field workers just coming from hostile labour negotiations; this is not a good time for them*	X		X		X	X

analysis comes from the total quality methods of the 1980s and it's been around so long, we aren't sure of the original source.

When to use. This assessment is useful when you suspect that certain stakeholders need to be engaged before you can be successful or when you need a way of summarizing the relative support that you have from each stakeholder.

How to prepare. Prepare a chart similar to that in Table 6.7 with just the first row completed.

Draw up a chart like Table 6.7. Then follow these steps:

1   List all of the important stakeholders down the left column.
2   Indicate with an X where each is now on the scale from 'make it happen' to 'stop it'.
3   Then indicate where you need each person or group to be for sustainability to move forward. Indicate that with an arrow. Note that sometimes you need people to be less supportive (e.g. when they are playing too strong a leadership role when others need to lead the effort).
4   For any group or individual whom you need to move, develop a strategy for doing so.

How to debrief. Develop action items for pursuing the strategies.

Table 6.7 *Sample stakeholder assessment*

Individual or group	Make it happen	Help it happen	Let it happen	Resist it from happening	Stop it from happening	Strategy
Plant manager	←————————X					Introduce him/her to other executives who are supportive of sustainability, especially customers
Labour union	X————→					Talk to union president and coach him or her to soften their approach
Florence in human resources			←————X			Give human resources research about the benefits of sustainability in attracting and retaining talented employees

Weighted criteria chart

You are likely to have more project ideas than time and money to do them. At the same time, you also have multiple criteria that matter to you. The human brain gets overloaded when it has too many options and criteria to consider simultaneously. In these situations, you need a method for considering each option against the list of criteria and then seeing which one comes out on top.

What follows is a description of a few options for doing this. The most common is a weighted criteria chart that allows you to score multiple options against multiple criteria. This can be used to rate project options. The Natural Step Scoring system is an example of how you can develop a simple scoring system tied to a specific sustainability framework. This can be used to identify high-impact problems to work on.

When to use. This is appropriate when you want to use a numerical method for choosing projects and the importance of your criteria vary widely and you want to reflect this.

How to prepare. Prepare a chart similar to Table 6.8 with your criteria listed along the left side. If you already have a list of possible projects, you can list these along the top. Otherwise, brainstorm possible projects to meet your goals in your meeting.

Table 6.8 *Sample weighted criteria chart*

	WEIGHT	Solar Panels	Variable speed motors	Window glazing	Compost bin
Payback	3	2 / 6	3 / 9	3 / 9	1 / 3
Feasibility	2	2 / 4	3 / 6	2 / 4	3 / 6
Leverage	3	1 / 3	3 / 9	1 / 3	1 / 3
Appeal	1	3 / 3	2 / 2	1 / 1	2 / 2
TOTAL		16	26	17	14

How to conduct this activity. Weighted criteria charts allow you to analyse a number of options against numerous variables that may have different levels of importance. Note that you may have done step 1 before the meeting:

1   In the left column, list your criteria. Along the top, list your options.
2   If your criteria have different levels of importance, assign a number between 1 and 3 (or 1 to 10) with the highest number being most important in the weight column and 1 being least important. If all your criteria are equally important, you can skip this step.
3   In the small boxes in each row, score each option on a 1 to 10 scale, indicating how well it meets the criteria, where 10 represents the best among the options for that criterion.
4   Multiply each score by the weight and put the resulting number in the larger boxes.
5   Add up these numbers in each column (the score times weight numbers).

If you identified and weighted the criteria well, the options with the highest scores best meet your needs.

How to debrief. Do a gut check on the results. Do they make sense? If your group has a strong negative reaction, it's possible that you ignored an important criterion. Otherwise, choose the projects with the highest scores and begin building a plan around them.

7

Developing Effective Management Systems[1]

CONCEPTS AND CASE EXAMPLES

When you implement sustainability or any other corporate initiative, you need a way of setting priorities, monitoring progress and reviewing the overall success of the effort. This process is often referred to as a 'management system'. This chapter will help you to examine the ways in which you currently manage initiatives and adapt them to include sustainability. We will show you how to evolve towards more mature and sophisticated processes for managing your sustainability initiative, what we are calling a sustainability management system (SMS).

While we use environmental management systems (EMSs) as a template, we avoid requirements for massive documentation and other disincentives sometimes associated with these systems. We believe that you can, over time, become more systematic as your situation warrants.

An effective SMS provides many of the following benefits. It helps organizations to:

- ensure that sustainability initiatives survive after key individuals move on;
- provide for regular tracking and reporting;
- provide a systemic framework for moving towards sustainability;
- become more proactive rather than reactive;
- transfer learning from project to project;
- reduce risks and liabilities;
- reduce confusion and overlapping or conflicting projects and priorities.

Four elements of a management system

Like all effective management systems, an SMS has four elements:

1 *Plan*: identify and select improvement projects.

2   *Implement*: launch the projects and develop appropriate support systems.
3   *Monitor*: check progress of the effort, monitor support systems, and take preventive and corrective action as needed.
4   *Review*: evaluate the effectiveness of the projects and the initiative overall.

Note that this process is sometimes referred to as plan–do–check–act; however, we've found that the terms plan–implement–monitor–review generate less confusion. The management system should simultaneously do two things:

1   Manage projects: manage the individual sustainability initiatives.
2   Manage the programme: manage the overall sustainability effort, including providing the support systems necessary.

Table 7.1 lays out these steps in a little more detail.

Table 7.1 *Tasks of a sustainability management system (SMS)*

Step	Manage projects	Manage the programme
Plan	Identify possible projects. Prioritize projects. Develop project plans.	Analyse the needs of the organization. Determine structures and support systems required. Create a sustainability plan and vision.
Implement	Launch projects. Conduct analysis. Take action.	Develop systems, including: • policies; • training; • communication; • document control; • emergency response; • corrective action; • measuring and reporting.
Monitor	Track the effectiveness of actions and adjust.	Audit critical systems. Gather feedback from stakeholders.
Review	Conduct a formal post-project review. Provide a formal report to management.	Conduct a formal review of the entire sustainability programme and produce a sustainability report.

BOX 7.1 WHAT IS AN ISO 14001 EMS?

ISO 14001 is the environmental management system (EMS) framework that was adopted by the International Organization for Standardization (ISO) in 1996. ISO is a worldwide federation of national standards bodies. The ISO 14001 standard was developed by an ISO technical committee (ISO/TC 207) and then adopted by the member bodies. It is not required by the US Environmental Protection Agency (EPA) or by any other regulatory agencies. Organizations adopt an EMS if they see the benefit. In some cases, such as the auto industry, companies give preference to vendors that have an ISO 14001 EMS. In other cases, a corporation makes a decision that all its facilities will implement an EMS. If a company follows the ISO 14001 format, it has the option to be certified by a third-party auditor. This process involves an initial certification audit to verify that the organization meets the requirements of the standard, followed by surveillance audits on a regular basis, usually every six months.

How do an EMS and SMS differ?

An EMS focuses on environmental issues such as improving environmental performance and regulatory compliance. An SMS has a broader focus and takes into account natural limits. It encompasses all of the components of sustainability – environmental, economic and social. An EMS often focuses on eco-efficiencies: doing better. An SMS takes a whole systems view and asks: are we doing enough to live within the limits of nature?

If you have an existing EMS, then the following checklist in Box 7.2 will help you to see where you can embed sustainability within it.

BOX 7.2 CONVERTING AN ENVIRONMENTAL MANAGEMENT SYSTEM (EMS) TO A SUSTAINABILITY MANAGEMENT SYSTEM (SMS): CHECKLIST

Plan

❑ *Policy.* Do you reference sustainability in the policy (e.g. TNS system conditions)?
❑ *Environmental impacts analysis.* Do you use sustainability screening criteria?
❑ *Setting objectives and targets.* Do these move you closer to being a sustainable organization?

Implement

❑ *Roles and responsibilities.* Is there an individual that is responsible for the SMS; do job descriptions include sustainability-related functions?

❏ *Training.* Does your training include sustainability awareness and understanding, in general, and what it means for your organization?

❏ *Standard operating procedures (SOPs)/operational control.* Is sustainability embedded within your SOPs? Do you use sustainability criteria to screen new materials, new processes, and activities?

Monitor

❏ *Monitoring and measurements.* Do you have metrics that have sustainability built into them?

❏ *SMS audits.* Do audit protocols use the sustainability framework?

Review

❏ *Management review.* Do you use your vision of your sustainable organization to enhance your strategic review?

Signs that you need a better management system

Some organizations have casual ways of managing initiatives and others have very disciplined, well-documented processes (e.g. quality management systems based on ISO 9000 or environmental management systems based on ISO 14000). While you don't necessarily need a system rigorous enough to meet ISO certification – a pizza restaurant requires a different degree of rigor than a nuclear power plant – you want to ensure that your sustainability initiative is sustainable itself! Without such a management system, you run the risk of launching a great first effort and then having the initiative die.

Have you encountered any of these situations (if you haven't implemented any sustainability-related projects, think about other corporate initiatives that you've applied in the past)?

If you have experienced any of these situations, you probably need to be more systematic about how you manage your sustainability initiative. Ultimately, an SMS integrates sustainability into everyday business operations; sustainability becomes part of the daily responsibility of all employees throughout the organization.

Different ways of achieving the same ends

Tables 7.3 to 7.6 correspond to each of the four components of the management system: plan, implement, monitor and review. In these charts, we define activities that you will

Table 7.2 *Self-assessment: Do you need a better management system?*

Situation	Yes	No
You have completed one successful incubator project, but have difficulty keeping the momentum going.		
There are only a couple of people who are taking the initiative to get projects going. If they leave, no more projects will be done.		
Sustainability is a project-by-project effort. It isn't integrated within the core business.		
You do a good job of getting projects planned and, basically, implemented, but don't check on how successful they are several months or a year later – to make sure that they are still working.		
You have had some really successful initiatives. Now you have lots of new project ideas, but have no systematic way of identifying and prioritizing what is really the most important to tackle next.		
Your stakeholders are asking questions about your results and you don't have coherent answers or the data to back them up.		

need to do (see the 'You need a way to …' column). Then we show how organizations often perform these activities based on their maturity level. We identify three different levels of maturity:

1 *Incubator phase*. This is the toe-testing phase when an organization is experimenting with the concept of sustainability but may not have made a formal public commitment to it. Sustainability projects are in addition to normal business responsibilities. Often, task forces or green teams are formed to explore opportunities.
2 *Initiative phase*. After some experimentation, organizations are ready to step up to the next level and make sustainability a formal initiative. Leaders talk about sustainability as one of a number of goals or initiatives that they are pursuing. Employees are trained and more formal systems are set up to manage the initiative.
3 *Integration phase*. Eventually, sustainability may become embedded in everything that the organization does. Sustainability becomes synonymous with your mission, so it is no longer split up from other goals. The organization doesn't have separate sustainability initiatives because everything is related to sustainability. At this point, pursuing sustainability is part of the normal business planning process, not something extra.

These tables are intended to show you how you might evolve towards a more systematic SMS. But you don't need to start with the Cadillac version. Find a system that fits the maturity level

Table 7.3 *Phases of development for planning*

Plan	How this is often done by maturity level		
You need a way to ...	Incubator phase	Initiative phase	Integration phase
Identify possible projects.	Look for project linked to something currently planned (e.g. constructing new buildings, developing a new product). Conduct cursory environmental impact assessment (see Chapter 4). Respond to a recent event (e.g. spike in energy prices, new regulation, non-compliance finding, customer pressure). Develop a list of possible projects.	Conduct systematic and disciplined impact assessment. Review business threats and opportunities. Review all legal/regulatory requirements and performance against them. Look at audits findings. Take ideas from employee suggestion system. Use recommendations from previous projects. Maintain a list of possible projects. Compare performance versus your environmental policy and sustainability targets (see Chapter 5).	Define a clear, compelling vision of your organization's role in a sustainable world (see Chapter 3). Develop strategic initiatives that expand your influence beyond the walls of your organization. Integrate within a core business planning process. Reframe your products as services. Regularly update and review impact analysis.
Prioritize and select the best projects.	Pick a quick win and a potential big win (see Chapter 6). Choose ones with symbolic value. Select ones with educational value.	Develop a systematic screening process using a holistic sustainability framework (e.g. The Natural Step) to select sustainability projects (see Chapter 3).	*All* projects are put through the sustainability screens. Use total cost accounting and life-cycle assessment to internalize external costs.
Develop an implementation plan for each project.	Identify a task force to work on the projects, as well as a steering committee to oversee multiple team efforts (see Chapter 8).	Build projects into the departmental plans, not as something extra.	Sustainability is so embedded within the organization that you can't separate these projects from any others.

Table 7.4 *Phases of development for implementing*

Implement	How this is often done by maturity level		
You need a way to ...	Incubator phase	Initiative phase	Integration phase
Implement projects.	Use a trained facilitator or consultant to guide the project teams. Write a charter for task forces (see Chapter 8). Ask for volunteers.	Move the responsibility for leading the projects to people inside your organization. Use more formal project management tools to manage the projects. Include key stakeholders as project team members.	Integrate projects within your normal departmental and business operations. Develop roles and responsibilities that fully integrate sustainability within your organization.
Develop support systems.	Identify training needs. Form a steering group to manage the incubator phase. Conduct sustainability awareness training for employees.	Rewrite job descriptions integrating routine sustainability functions. Prepare standard operating procedures for sustainability activities. Start a comprehensive sustainability training programme; train people in new procedures. Assign someone to take leadership role (at least part time). Develop a communication system and strategy (newsletters, web sites, etc.). Develop documentation and information systems.	Include sustainability training in regular employee training programme. Communicate internally and externally on efforts. Refine control systems to ensure that accurate and up-to-date information is available (e.g. web-based information, removal of out-of-date policies and procedures). Integrate sustainability within new employee orientation. Appoint/hire someone to lead the sustainability effort (typically full time).

of your sustainability effort and your organization's size. We will provide you with instructions for using these tables in the 'Methods and instructions' section of this chapter.

Note that as your SMS becomes more sophisticated, your focus moves from managing individual projects to managing the overall management system.

Table 7.5 *Phases of development for monitoring*

Monitor	How this is often done by maturity level		
You need a way to...	Incubator phase	Initiative phase	Integration phase
Track how your projects are going.	Hire experts or consultants to meet regularly with team leaders, the steering committee and management. Gather pre- and post-data for projects.	Develop procedures for consistent data collection.	Track projects as part of your normal responsibilities of all managers.
Track how your systems are working.	Implement consultant recommendations. Establish a suggestion system. Respond to problems.	Gather baseline measures in most/all sustainability metrics. Establish and collect routine measures for ongoing sustainability activities. Develop a more formal suggestion system or preventive/corrective action system. Start a systems audit programme.	Conduct regular system audits. Encourage everyone to contribute to SMS improvement with an active preventive and corrective action system.

Tips for creating a management system

- Think about who will manage the management system. This is usually best done by a single person or single department that has enough oversight within the organization to see across functions and processes.
- Make sure your management system is robust enough to spot and account for the 'multiple benefits' effect often associated with sustainability efforts in which a project implemented to improve or save one thing ends up having positive benefits in other areas or other departments as well.

RESOURCES

- *Environmental management systems.* The US Environmental Protection Agency (EPA) has developed an EMS website (www.epa.gov/ems) that describes some of the various programmes that the EPA is implementing which promote EMS. In addition, this site contains publications and policies available from EPA.

- *Standards publications.* The American National Standards Institute (ANSI) coordinates the development of American National Standards and is one of five permanent members of the governing ISO council. ANSI sells copies of the ISO 14000 standards (see http://web.ansi.org/).
- *International Organization for Standardization (ISO).* ISO developed the ISO 14001 series of standards, guidance documents and technical reports, including the ISO 14001 EMS standard (see www.iso.org).
- *American Society for Testing and Materials (ASTM).* ASTM is an authorized distributor of the ISO standards (see www.astm.org).
- *NSF International.* NSF is an authorized distributor of the ISO standards (see www.nsf.org).

Table 7.6 *Phases of development for reviewing*

Review	How this is often done by maturity level		
You need a way to ...	Incubator phase	Initiative phase	Integration phase
Review the status and results of individual projects.	Project members' report status, results and lessons learned to the steering committee. Management sponsors check in with the teams on a regular basis and/or participate on the teams.	Project members' report status, results and lessons learned to the steering committee and/or management.	Project members' report status, results and lessons learned through normal management channels. SMS review team to review projects as part of its normal periodic (quarterly/annual) review.
Review the SMS and the entire sustainability effort.	Steering committee makes recommendations to management on how to move forward.	Create top management SMS review team (steering committee with top management represented). SMS review team meets to review overall results, and reports to top management. Publish sustainability or corporate social responsibility report (see Chapter 5).	Top management SMS review team conducts regular (quarterly/annual) strategic review of SMS, which includes policy, metrics, objectives, audit results and new priorities. Publish results in either the annual report and/or a Global Reporting Initiative-compliant sustainability report.

METHODS AND INSTRUCTIONS

In this section, we explain five activities or processes that are helpful in developing better systems for managing sustainability.

Sustainability policy

When to use. Many organizations write a formal policy related to sustainability that is approved by the board of directors or in government, the city council or other appropriate body. The following process will help you to draft language that can be used in your policy document.

How to prepare. List the following questions on a board or flip chart. If possible, assemble some sustainability policies from other organizations. Bring copies or prepare to project them for all to see.

How to conduct this activity:

1   Explain the purpose of a sustainability policy. It is to set direction, making clear the commitment and intent of the organization relative to sustainability.
2   Review some typical examples and talk about what you like and don't like.
3   Talk through the following questions, making notes as you go. Then have someone try to weave the most cogent points into a draft (this can often be done over a short break):
   •   What are you striving to achieve?
   •   What is the unique contribution that your organization can make to solve sustainability challenges?
   •   What do you want to become known for?

Table 7.7 *Overview of methods for creating a management system*

Process	When to use
Policy statement	Help draft a sustainability policy.
Sustainability management system (SMS) improvement opportunities	Analyse the strengths and weaknesses of your systems and brainstorm ways of improving your SMS.
SMS process summary	Document the major responsibilities for your SMS. Most useful after the SMS improvement opportunities.
Gap analysis	Audit your existing SMS. Most useful for more mature SMSs (initiative and integrated phases).
Formal management review	Conduct a formal executive review of your sustainability system.

- Are there certain sustainability frameworks you intend to use?
- Are there any existing corporate documents that you can link to this vision (e.g. mission, values, strategic plans, etc.)?
- Is there a date by which you intend to be fully sustainable?
- Is there a 'bumper-sticker' phrase that would make your vision easy to remember?

4   Find out reactions to the draft and refine it.
5   Get formal approval for the policy from the appropriate management body after the meeting.

SMS improvement opportunities

When to use. This exercise helps you to analyse the information in Tables 7.3 to 7.6.
  How to prepare. You may find the following SMS worksheet in Table 7.8 helpful.

Table 7.8 *SMS worksheet*

You need a way to …	How we did this in the past	Results	Problems	Next time	Timing/ frequency
Plan					
Identify possible projects.					
Prioritize and select projects.					
Develop an implementation plan.					
Implement					
Implement projects.					
Develop support systems.					
Monitor					
Track how your projects are going.					
Track how your systems are working.					
Review					
Review the status of individual projects.					
Review the SMS and the entire sustainability effort.					

How to conduct this activity:

1   First, glance down the left column of Tables 7.3 to 7.6 to get a sense of the scope of an SMS ('You need a way to ...' column).
2   Then select the maturity level of your sustainability effort (incubator, initiative or integration) and review that column. If you're just beginning, you're probably in the incubator phase; if you have been working on sustainability-related projects for over a year, the initiative phase might be more appropriate. If you have had an ISO-compliant EMS, the integration column is most likely to suit your situation.
3   Find at least one way of meeting each need (row). Check any practices that you have used in the past (for sustainability or any other improvement initiative). Circle any that look like good enhancements to your existing practices (you need to have at least one method in each row).
4   Review the next column to the right, one maturity level up, to get ideas about longer-term improvements that you could make to your management system. Circle any that look like logical next steps.

SMS process summary

When to use. Use the worksheet in Table 7.9 to document your decisions about how your SMS should perform each of the tasks.

   How to prepare. Create a chart similar to the one in Table 7.9 with the top row and left column completed. Leave the rest of the chart blank. We provide a completed sample in Table 7.9. Note that we have shaded boxes that relate to managing the system (versus individual initiatives.)

   How to conduct this activity. Assemble the appropriate people and together complete the boxes in the 'how', 'when' and 'who' columns.

Gap analysis

When to use. When you want to assess the effectiveness of your SMS and make improvements.

   How to prepare. Bring a document that summarizes your existing SMS and create a chart as in Table 7.10.

   How to conduct this activity. Follow these steps to audit your systems:

1   Divide the system up into logical parts. You may choose to use the structure in our tables in this chapter (You need a way to ...) or you may choose to audit each element of ISO 14001. The gap analysis worksheet in Table 7.10 assumes the latter.

Table 7.9 *Sample SMS process summary*

	What	How	When	Who
Plan	Gather ideas for action.	Solicit ideas from all employees.	September	Steering committee; managers
	Decide what to work on.	Review all ideas, including those from the suggestion box, and use weighted criteria chart to choose the best.	October	Steering committee
	Develop an implementation plan for all significant projects/actions.	Develop an annual implementation plan with milestones.	November	Steering committee; get approval from top management.
	Identify support systems that need to be developed or enhanced.	Develop an annual implementation plan with milestones.	November	Steering committee; get approval from top management
Implement	Charter teams or assign responsibility.	Assign each project either to an existing person/function or charter a task force.	January	Assigned individuals/departments and task forces as appropriate
	Implement the projects/actions.	Gather baseline data, identify options, choose the best options and implement.	January–June	Assigned individuals/departments and task forces as appropriate
	Implement improvements to support systems.	Assign each project either to an existing person/function or charter a task force.	February	Assigned individuals/departments and task forces as appropriate
Monitor	Monitor progress of sustainability projects.	Have each task force and assigned individual provide a verbal progress report to the steering committee.	March–September	Steering committee along with assigned individuals/departments and task forces as appropriate

Table 7.9 Sample SMS process summary (Cont'd)

	What	How	When	Who
	Gather data and material for the annual sustainability report.	Assemble performance data and produce the report.	September	Steering committee
	Monitor the effectiveness of improvements to your support systems.	Quarterly, have each task force and assigned individual provide a verbal progress report to the steering committee.	March, June and September	Steering committee along with assigned individuals/ departments and task forces as appropriate
Review	Conduct a formal review of sustainability projects.	Deliver to top management a report for this year and a plan for next year (note that this happens simultaneously with part of 'planning' above).	October	Steering committee, Sustainability director
		Prepare a draft public sustainability report for executive approval.	January–February	Sustainability director
	Incorporate lessons learned within policies and practices.	Institutionalize lessons learned.	November–December	Managers as appropriate
	Audit the SMS.	Plan and conduct the audit and review findings.	November–December	Sustainability director and employees trained as auditors
	Conduct a formal review of SMS	(Conducted at the same time as the formal review of sustainability projects.)		

Table 7.10 *Gap analysis worksheet*

ISO 14001 element	Criteria (and scoring)	Audit score	Observations	Recommendations
1 Environmental policy				
2 Environmental aspects				
3 Legal and other requirements				
4 Objectives and targets				
5 Environmental management programme				
6 Structure and responsibility				
7 Training, awareness and competency				
8 Communication				
9 EMS documentation				
10 Document control				
11 Operational control				
12 Emergency response				
13 Monitoring and measurement				
14 Corrective and preventive action				
15 Records				
16 Audits				
17 Management review				

2   Look at each part and define criteria that would determine whether it is functioning or not. Define a scoring system (e.g. 1 to 5; high, medium, low; unsatisfactory, meets, exceeds).

3   Develop questions and a list of documents/records that will help to determine if it is functioning.

4   Identify and train a group of people to conduct the audit. They should look at documents and interview people as appropriate.

5   Do the audit.

6   Compile the results and recommendations.

7   Communicate results and recommendations to management and other relevant parties.

8   Take action to correct any deficiencies.

Formal management review

When to use. Management should conduct a strategic review of the sustainability effort on a regular basis. This involves reviewing the status and lessons from ongoing sustainability projects, as well as reflecting on the effectiveness of the SMS support systems that support these projects.

How to prepare. Check in with all of those working on sustainability efforts to see if they have results or challenges that they'd like to share. Gather any necessary performance data and summarize progress on last year's goals. If appropriate, prepare a short presentation or packet summarizing the results.

How to conduct this activity. Use the following agenda to gather the pertinent review data:

- Follow up on items from the previous SMS review meeting.
- Review status of ongoing sustainability projects – objectives and targets.
- Evaluate the list of potential sustainability projects for possible new ones.
- Review the log of corrective and preventive action requests/suggestions.
- Review external communications and follow-ups.
- Review SMS audit findings.
- Evaluate the functioning of the overall management system – identify improvement opportunities.
- Assign action items and set the next meeting time.

NOTE

1   This chapter is adapted from Hitchcock and Atwood (2002).

8

Determining the Structures Needed to Manage the Effort[1]

CONCEPTS AND CASE EXAMPLES

Now that you have a plan in place, it's time to think about what structures will be needed to support the plan. In the ideal world, the management team would be ready and willing to integrate sustainability within their efforts; but this is not often the case starting out. Instead, organizations often need such 'parallel' management structures as steering committees to focus on a new initiative. In addition, since sustainability is about the whole system, organizations often need cross-functional task forces to work on sustainability issues that cross over typical organizational boundaries. Frequently, organizations create a new position (sustainability director or coordinator) and staff it with someone who can coordinate or direct the whole effort. Thinking through these structures also helps you to more effectively manage the stakeholders that need to be involved and ensure that there are easy ways for employees to become engaged. This chapter helps you to determine what kinds of structures will be most useful and what methods work best with each.

Most organizations migrate to a model that looks a bit like Figure 8.1.

A sustainability coordinator, executive sponsor or sustainability director heads the programme. This individual chairs a steering committee that oversees the implementation of sustainability. The steering committee often spawns temporary task forces (or sometimes sets up standing teams) that work on specific areas or projects.

Eventually, this temporary structure should evaporate as sustainability becomes part of the normal role of management and their staff. But this structure has worked successfully in many different organizational change initiatives.

Sustainability director/coordinator responsibilities

While everyone agrees that they want sustainability to be part of everyone's job, the reality is that most organizations need someone whose job focuses on shepherding the effort. This

Figure 8.1 *Common structures for managing sustainability*

may be a part-time or full-time job, based on the size of the organization. But few organizations get far without one. Typically, the sustainability director or coordinator is responsible for the following tasks:

- *Chair or facilitate the steering committee.* Plan meetings, manage the agendas, prepare materials for the meetings and facilitate the meetings.
- *Manage and monitor the change process.* Keep a focus on sustainability; develop effective strategies for moving forward that fit the culture, priorities and constraints of the organization; help departments to overcome barriers and resistance; provide consulting assistance to those who need it; look for and act on 'teachable moments'.
- *Be a resource.* Have a general knowledge of sustainability concepts, frameworks, issues, tools and resources; provide minor technical assistance and refer people to appropriate resources for complex technical needs.
- *Inspire others.* Develop enthusiasm and support for sustainability at all levels of the organization; provide mechanisms for teaching staff about relevant concepts, methods and tools.
- *Draft documents.* Create 'strawdog' versions of sustainability-related documents. This may include council and administrative policies, sustainability implementation plans, sustainability management system elements, checklists and job aids, as well as language for job descriptions, contracts and performance reviews.
- *Facilitate progress.* Develop processes and tools that the steering committee and departments can use to set goals, implement plans and institutionalize learning. Provide assistance in using them.

- *Ensure that the sustainability management system (SMS) is working.* As the steering committee develops elements of a sustainability management system, ensure that plans are completed, reviews are conducted, goals are enacted, etc.
- *Communicate.* This may include updating the city's website, writing articles for the *Read and Recycle* newsletters, speaking to groups internally and externally, and being the primary contact for sustainability issues, ideas and requests.
- *Prepare the annual sustainability report.* Develop a template for the sustainability report, solicit content, track sustainability metrics, produce the report and communicate results.

While we would never argue against having a sustainability director, there are some things to watch for. As we learned during the last century in the Total Quality Management Movement, when organizations were learning to focus on product and service quality, vesting one person with the title of 'sustainability director' can leave the rest of the members of your organization feeling like someone else is taking care of the problem and that it is not their responsibility to attend to or participate in the initiative. Sustainability is a systems issue and, as such, is most effective when it is embedded within the fabric of the organization. As long as it resides in the sustainability director's office, people might mistakenly assume that it's not part of their job. The sustainability director needs to encourage and facilitate involvement, not try to do it all alone. It might, in some cases, be wise to frame the job as temporary, with the expectation of turning over responsibility for sustainability to the management team in five to ten years. We are too early into the evolution of sustainability to know whether this position will need to become a long-term executive job or a transitional one.

Steering committee responsibilities

Steering committees are parallel management structures commonly used to implement new corporate initiatives. They provide a way for organizations to strategize about implementation outside the formal management structure. Steering committees are usually sponsored by an executive and operate within that person's span of influence. They set priorities, launch and oversee task forces, and make strategic decisions regarding the implementation of sustainability (e.g. what frameworks to use, where to begin and how to measure success). Eventually you want the work of the steering committee to migrate into the normal management channels.

Steering committees usually work best under the following circumstances:

- Their membership is designed carefully. Often they include a 'diagonal slice' of the organization; some members may be volunteers, but they often may include specific individuals whose position is key to the effort. For example, the facilities manager or purchasing manager may be crucial to the steering committee's success. It is also important to have at least one member of the organization's leadership or decision-making team.

- They make use of a facilitator who has experience with sustainability steering committees and implementation.
- They actively communicate with and ask for input from their constituents.

BOX 8.1 TASKS OF A SUSTAINABILITY STEERING COMMITTEE

Analysis. Typically, a steering committee will undertake many of the analytical tasks covered in this book. This may include the following:

- Take a whole systems view of the organization
- Refine the business case
- Decide on sustainability framework(s), language and definitions
- Analyze impacts
- Build a framework and systems for managing sustainability projects
- Conduct sustainability assessments

Implementation. A steering committee is often helpful in guiding the decisions about when, where and how to begin the sustainability effort. These tasks may include the following:

- Decide where to start and what to link this to.
- Create a communication plan and process.
- Plan and offer sustainability-related education.
- Coach management to walk the talk and demonstrate their support.
- Recommend ways to embed sustainability within business systems.

Recurrent tasks. Year after year, the steering committee typically manages the sustainability effort. While these tasks could be done by a sustainability director or coordinator, they would lack the organizational buy-in without the broad involvement that a steering committee can provide. These tasks usually include the following:

- Set priorities.
- Charter, launch and support task forces.
- Build and track sustainability metrics.
- Monitor and remove barriers to success.
- Develop a sustainability plan (short, intermediate and long term).
- Produce an annual sustainability report.
- Report to top management.
- Advise top management on sustainability developments and opportunities.
- Communicate results to appropriate stakeholders.

BOX 8.2 SIMPLOT'S EVOLVING STEERING COMMITTEE

Roughly a decade ago the Don Plant in Pocatello, which produces agricultural feed compounds, began its pollution prevention efforts with a committee of over 20 people made up of representatives from each department. The committee was in some ways too large to be effective; but it was a way to provide involvement of all areas. The committee would pick an issue such as eliminating aerosol cans and then each member would go back to their area and explore with the workers how that goal might be accomplished.

The steering committee evolved from an unwieldy team to one with a handful of well-positioned individuals, including two of their five senior managers, a member of the lab (a research function), a purchasing agent, an environmental representative, and representatives from maintenance and planning. They also have seats for rank-and-file employees who rotate on and off the team. Together, when they decide to move in a direction, they have the clout to make it happen. As Scott Harris, laboratory analyst, explains, the team is made up of critical functions. The laboratory represents the design function; most of the impacts of anything are determined in the design phase. Purchasing controls what comes into the plant. Maintenance and planning decide how things get done and how waste is handled. The two senior managers act as a link pin to the senior management team, pushing through their recommendations at that level. Just like the former steering committee, this one sets priorities or goals and then actively solicits ideas from employees about how to improve operations. Scott says: 'Many of the things we do are because they're the right thing to do. But then, when we look back, we discover that we actually saved money doing it.' Tracking and communicating those savings is crucial to maintaining management support. Scott can tell you how much they saved on eliminating aerosol cans and their variable frequency drives. Turning excess steam into energy has saved US$5 million per year, offsetting enough power to serve 8000 homes. To get around the plant, they use bicycles and motorized 'mules', reducing their fuel consumption by 35 per cent and potentially improving the health of employees.

Teams

Teams are a common way of involving a good number of employees in sustainability efforts. Most of these teams (with the possible exception of voluntary green teams) are formally sanctioned efforts by the organization, giving them legitimacy. Sustainable solutions often require an interdisciplinary multi-stakeholder approach, involving people from across the organization or even from multiple organizations. So, teams are the most common way of getting the right mix of people into a room together.

Any team effort will benefit from the following advice:

• Before you launch the team, think carefully about who should be on the team, what its purpose is and what its boundaries are. Where possible, define the boundaries so clearly that the team has the power to choose and implement at least some ideas. See the 'Team pre-launch' section in this chapter to create a clear team charter *before* forming any team.

- Since many people already feel overwhelmed with work, consult with managers to ensure that the team members are granted the time to participate in team meetings and do any other work associated with the team. Be clear up front about the time involved and the duration of the commitment.
- To get the most out of the meetings, provide a trained facilitator for the team meetings and make full use of group problem-solving and decision-making tools.
- Put in place a process for coordinating and evaluating the recommendations of the teams.
- Set the meeting length to match the needs of the work to be done. Teams that agree to meet, for example, one hour a week or month, typically lose momentum. Time is wasted in meetings recalling the results of the previous meeting. Members leave. Instead, think of the team meetings as a process. What are the main steps or tasks that will need to be done? Some meetings may need to be longer than others.

In Table 8.1 we describe different types of teams and how they operate. Some teams are hybrids; but it's important to understand which type of team you have and how it affects its membership and activities.

All of these teams serve a useful function. It's important to match your choice of team type with the readiness of your organization and the purpose you intend for it. It's not uncommon for organizations to begin with a voluntary green team, which then evolves into a steering committee that fulfils a more strategic management-sanctioned role. When that happens, they often have to adjust the membership of the team as it is no longer enough to leave membership up to serendipity; certain key roles (e.g. purchasing, facilities or a union) may have to be represented. As your teams evolve, take time to consider how their role is changing and what impacts that may have on the team's membership and operation.

Voluntary teams. 'Green teams' often start out as voluntary teams that meet during off-work hours (e.g. over lunch). These teams frequently do not have much formal standing in the organization. However, they provide a way, typically early in the implementation of sustainability, for people who have enthusiasm to meet and explore possibilities. These teams can help to build support for sustainability within the organization. Usually, organizations transition from green teams to one of the more formal sanctioned team structures below.

Green teams benefit from the following advice:

- Be sensitive to the readiness of your organization. Be careful not to come across as zealots. Work to frame your efforts in language that will make sense to the rest of the organization. Focus on bottom-line business results.
- Since membership is voluntary, spend some time clarifying shared expectations.

Table 8.1 *Types of teams and when each is useful*

Voluntary 'green' teams	Purpose: typically to expand awareness and build support for a more strategic effort. Often these teams host brownbag speakers' series, green fairs and other awareness-building events. They may also attempt to change the operation of the organization, usually in small ways (e.g. eliminating Styrofoam cups in the lunch room).
	Membership: voluntary – whoever wants to join.
	Authority: very limited; the team is permitted by management often, in part, because the team meets during non-work time and has no budget.
Task forces	Purpose: to carry out a specific short-term project (e.g. conduct a waste audit, design a transportation incentive programme, etc.).
	Membership: often members are chosen based on their relevant knowledge for the particular task.
	Authority: have the power to decide or recommend improvements within their charter. They usually report to a steering committee or a management team.
Standing teams	Purpose: similar to a task force but they are 'permanent'. They may be organized around specific aspects or impacts of an organization (water, energy, purchasing, etc.).
	Membership: often members rotate on and off these standing teams.
	Authority: typically recommend improvements to a steering committee or management team.

- Move quickly to find tangible tasks for the team to perform that are likely to be approved by management.
- Often, the best role for the green team is outreach and to educate others about the issues and solutions.

Box 8.3 CH2M HILL: A GREEN TEAM WITH GUSTO

Brandy Wilson and Betsy Roberts headed up a green team in the Boise, ID office for CH2M HILL, a large engineering firm, after being inspired by a similar effort in other offices. Membership was entirely voluntary and the team had no official authority to make decisions. Making time for the green team can be tough in the CH2M HILL culture, which emphasizes billable hours. Yet, they were still able to make a significant impact, in part by being strategic about their actions. They focused on initiatives that could save the office money, including initiatives around energy and waste. In their five years, they have done a lot! This is only a partial list:

- Installed automatic sensor lights in common areas and conference rooms that shut off the lights when not in use.
- Installed higher-efficiency light bulbs and ballasts.
- Recycled white paper and coloured paper.
- Purchased only pale-yellow post-its because those can be recycled; bright colours cannot.
- Set printers in the office to default double-sided printing.
- Used alternative report delivery methods, such as web sites, CD-ROMs and other electronic means.
- Donated old computers and printers instead of 'trashing' them (e.g. to schools and programmes for disadvantaged kids).
- Collected batteries and light bulbs; they are taken to the solid waste collection facility instead of being thrown away.
- Installed recycled-material carpet squares throughout the building.
- Used low volatile organic compound (VOC) paints to reduce pollution and improve indoor air health.
- Cleaned and rebalanced the entire heating/air-conditioning system, which improved equipment efficiency, resulted in energy savings and enhanced the staff's working environment.

As part of building the business case for making pollution prevention a higher priority, one person tallied the number of times requests for proposals (RFPs) asked for evidence of an environmental management system. This data showed their management that their customers did care about 'green' efforts. They now have an organization-wide environmental management system (that Brandy now manages) with several years of data recorded and trended.

The green team also found ways of involving people who didn't come to meetings. For example, they hosted an event to 'green' the Christmas holiday. Employees who hadn't attended a single meeting came prepared to teach people about little things they had done. One woman, for example, demonstrated how she took the scraps left over from peel-off label sheets to make gift tags. Another showed how to wrap presents with old topographic maps. This event gave employees a way to be involved and demonstrate their creativity and commitment to sustainability.

The green team has also leveraged programmes that their customers have. For example, their local county government, one of their major clients, has a programme to encourage alternative transportation, so the green team has set a goal of beating the county at their own game! This is one way of demonstrating their alignment with the county's goals and culture.

Task forces. Task forces are temporary teams assembled to perform a specific task (e.g. to conduct a solid waste audit and recommend improvements or to create the sustainability metrics that will be included in sustainability reports). These task forces usually are created by and report to either a steering committee or management.

Task forces benefit from the following advice:

- Before the task force is formed, the sponsors should create a carefully crafted charter for them. Why is the team being formed? What exactly is it expected to do and how will success be measured? What does the task force have authority to decide? What boundaries must their decisions and recommendations live within? Who needs to be on the team or how will membership be determined? See the 'Team pre-launch' section later in this chapter.
- It is helpful to make use of a facilitator who has experience with the task that the team has been given so they don't waste time figuring out what to do.
- Task forces often work best when they allocate a few long meetings rather than meeting for just an hour a week. The timeframes should match the steps in their process. For example, a task force might have an hour-long formation meeting with their sponsor(s), and a four-hour meeting to analyse options and priorities. Then there may be a period when people investigate different options. The team members may share the results via email and then meet for another four hours to choose a course of action and develop a plan for action.
- Teams shouldn't get too far down any path without checking with their sponsor(s) and appropriate stakeholders.
- Provide a way for employees to submit suggestions to the task force. Have a system for responding to all suggestions promptly.

Standing teams. Standing teams are intended to be permanent (as permanent as anything is in our organizations these days!). Their purpose is to seek ways of continuously improving sustainability performance. Some organizations organize these teams around issues (e.g. climate change, solid waste, etc.). Others organize around processes (see Box 8.4). Other alternatives include organizing around job function (so that everyone who does a particular job meets periodically) or workgroup/department.

If you implement standing teams, keep these suggestions in mind:

- Choose a logical organization for the teams that makes sense for your organization, ensures that all-important areas of focus are covered, and has the potential to generate other benefits (e.g. convening people who do the same job in dispersed geographic locations may facilitate the exchange of many improvement ideas, not just those related to sustainability).
- Have a process and structure in place to manage the ideas that these teams generate. Recommendations should be reviewed by a management team or steering committee to ensure that scarce funds are used to the best advantage. This also ensures that actions taken by the teams fit into long-term plans for the organization.

BOX 8.4 COLLINS COMPANY'S SUSTAINABILITY TEAM STRUCTURE

Collins Company is a vertically integrated forest/wood products business. They were the first in the US to have all of their forests Forest Stewardship Council (FSC) certified as sustainably harvested. They produce lumber and engineered wood products. When they implemented sustainability in their Klamath Falls, Oregon, plant, they quickly realized that just training people wasn't enough to create action. So they organized standing teams around their work process.

They formed a team for each of their primary inputs (energy and materials) and their major outputs (products and waste.). They also formed teams for their emissions (water and air), as well as their link to their community (e.g. through their Adopt a Highway programme).

Once these standing teams were in place, tangible ideas for improvement began to flow that have saved the company millions of dollars per year. However, Collins quickly realized that they needed to link these teams to their formal management structure. Otherwise, these teams were making decisions unbeknownst to their plant manager! So now the teams report to a steering committee (what they call their core team) that includes key individuals in the management team. The core team requires a form to be completed for all capital projects.

RESOURCES

- One of AXIS Performance Advisors' *Sustainability Series*™ booklets covers how to choose the type of team you'll need and provides best practices for each. It also includes instructions on some of the most useful group process facilitation tools. *Forming and Facilitating Sustainability Teams: Steering Committees to Task Forces* is available from the AXIS website: www.axisperformance.com.
- About.com is a site full of articles and recommendations. Check out the pages devoted to human resource issues and green teams, in particular: http://humanresources.about.com/od/employeeinvolvement/qt/work_environs.htm

Other good facilitation resources include:

- Hackett, D. W. and Martin, C. (1993) Crisp: *Facilitation Skills for Team Leaders – Leading Organized Teams to Greater Productivity*, Crisp Fifty-Minute Series, Crisp Learning, Mississauga, Ontario, Canada
- Justice, T. and Jamieson, D. (2006) *The Facilitator's Fieldbook,* second edition, HRD Press, New York, NY
- Schwarz, R., Davidson, A., Carlson, P. and McKinney, S. (2005) *The Skilled Facilitator Fieldbook*, Jossey Bass, San Francisco, CA

METHODS AND INSTRUCTIONS

In this section, we explain five activities or processes that are helpful in designing structures and launching teams.

Sustainability structure

When to use. Follow these instructions to determine the best set of structures to help you manage your sustainability efforts.

How to prepare. Convene a group of people who have authority to affect the structure of the organization.

How to conduct this activity. This process tries to leverage existing roles that you already have in your organization but can easily be modified to start with a clean slate if this is more appropriate:

1   Brainstorm tasks that will need to be done to support sustainability. Put one idea on each post-it note.
2   Review the tasks and cluster them into logical groupings (where you'd want the same person or group to do them), eliminating duplicates as you go along. If needed, put simple labels on stacks of post-its, preferably starting with an action verb (decide, approve, implement, etc.).
3   Diagram your existing structures on a flip chart or whiteboard that relate in some way to sustainability. These should include the management team and a sustainability

Table 8.2 *Overview of methods for developing structures*

Process	When to use
Sustainability structure	Determine the structures needed to support your sustainability efforts.
Responsibility list	Clarify responsibilities, especially decision authority.
Team pre-launch	Before you start any new team.
Team review agenda	Conduct a formal team review. Use after the conclusion of any temporary team (e.g. project team or task force) or periodically for any permanent or longstanding team.
Critical incident analysis	Uncover root causes and lessons learned from a specific incident or experience (good or bad). This is most often used to uncover the root causes of a problem that had far-reaching and/or emotional impacts.

director/coordinator if you have one. It may also include teams related to environmental management systems and existing steering committees, as well as, perhaps, pollution prevention or safety committees that might be directed to include sustainability in their mission. If you already know that you want to add certain structures, such as steering committees or task forces, add these to the chart. Use lines to show reporting relationships and any key individuals (e.g. executive sponsors).

4   Move the post-its to the existing structures. Which person or group is well positioned, willing and able to do each set of tasks?

5   Look at the tasks that are left. Can any be added to the existing structures? If not, discuss what type of entity might be appropriate to take on those tasks. If you create a new team or role, re-examine all of the other assignments to see if any should be moved around.

6   Cross-check these tasks with your sustainability management system (in Chapter 7) to make sure that you haven't forgotten anything.

7   Create a diagram that clearly shows the roles, groups and major responsibilities.

8   If needed, create a responsibility list (see below).

Responsibility list

When to use. Use this worksheet to clarify the responsibilities of each party involved in your sustainability effort (see Table 8.3).

How to prepare. Create a chart that explains each of the levels of involvement.

Use this legend:

- R = responsible;
- A = approve;
- I = have input.

Table 8.3 *Sample responsibility list*

Task/party	Steering committee	Executive team	Sustainability director	Task force(s)
Set priorities for each year.				
Manage the employee suggestion system, gathering ideas for action, working with employees to refine the ideas.	R		I	I
Evaluate ideas and determine priorities for next year.	R	A	I	

How to conduct this activity. We provide a partially completed sample in Table 8.3:

1   List the parties in the column headings.
2   List the tasks in the left column.
3   Determine the responsibilities for each task using the legend above.

Team pre-launch

When to use. This is appropriate at the launch of each of the teams or committees that you charter. One of the biggest mistakes that managers make regarding teams is to form them without careful thought. This leads to frustration and wasted time. We invented this team pre-launch process back when we were doing work with self-directed work teams; but it is just as valuable now.

How to prepare. When we tell a manager the process usually takes four hours, they are incredulous. How could such a simple act take so darn long? We always say that they're probably more prepared than most and suggest that they block out four hours anyway. If we get done early, we tell them, all the better. Invariably, 3 hours and 45 minutes into the session, they are still scrambling to finish the process and have a much clearer understanding of the complexity involved.

How to conduct this activity. The pre-launch is basically a process for creating a team charter. Many people like to leave the process of creating a charter to those who come together on the team; but in organizations, this often leads to problems. Because form should follow function, we prefer to involve people who think a team is needed to define a charter, at least a preliminary one. People will know what they are being asked to join:

1   Assemble the people who want to form a team, particularly the key executive/management sponsor and a few other key individuals. Do not try to assemble the individuals you expect to have on the team. Instead, invite key people who should be involved in determining the purpose of the team.
2   Create a copy of the following principles and worksheets. Someone can use these to take notes as you facilitate the meeting. Create flipcharts as you go, set up in the same fashion.
3   Explain the purpose of the meeting and review the principles upon which the process is based.
4   Why do you need a team? You want to answer this question both from the organization's perspective as well as the perspective of the individual team members. What is the background that led up to needing one? What's in it for the organization? What's in it for the team members too? You will use the organizational reasons for the team to explain the purpose. Use the insights about what team members might want to inform how you staff and operate the team. For example, if one of the reasons that

team members might want to participate is to expand their leadership skills, then you might provide opportunities for developing these skills on the team and mention this benefit when you invite people. You might decide to rotate responsibilities to facilitate team meetings, lead task forces or report to management.

5   What? Here you want to provide both a simple description of their task and clarify expectations. Identify a measurable goal related to the team's purpose (e.g. develop a plan that will reduce our solid waste to landfill by 50 per cent in three years). Don't be afraid of setting radical stretch goals; but tie them to external factors (e.g. system conditions and customer requirements) – not management whims.

Next, define what they are to do. We find the best way to do this is often to list questions that they will need to answer. For example, what are our major sources of waste? What is the next best use for each of those waste streams? What options do we have to divert major waste categories from the landfill? What costs or savings could be involved? Describe measures of success. How would you know if the team was successful?

Clarify the boundary conditions: what powers the team has. We usually explain that we are trying to describe the 'box' within which the team must stay. If you define the boundaries well, you should be able to give the team the power to decide, not just recommend. A team can push on one of the walls of the box; but it doesn't have the authority to make changes outside of the box. Often the best way to uncover these boundaries is to imagine that all of the stakeholders are around the table. What would each one say that would be unacceptable? Usually boundaries include such items as legal/regulatory demands, existing corporate systems, union agreements, spending/ budget limits, etc.

6   Who? Now that you know why the team is being formed and what it needs to do, you can turn your attention to membership. In some cases you may need to specify certain individuals (e.g. the facilities manager); in other situations you may be able to specify the characteristics of the individual (e.g. someone who knows how to operate the purchasing computer system). Don't limit yourself to people inside the organization; sometimes customers and suppliers can be useful core or non-core team members. Decide how people will be selected or invited onto the team. For example, if each department is to send a representative, how will that selection process work and what advice or criteria do you want to give each department as they decide on their representative? If they are acting as representatives, be sure to discuss how to keep those represented informed and involved. Also be clear about the level of commitment you are expecting. How long will someone be expected to serve on the team and how much time will it take?

7   When and where? Think about the logistics; how often/long should they meet? What milestones or deadlines do they have? Will they need access to facilities, people or budgets? Task forces seem to work best with short timeframes and intense work sessions (rather than meeting one hour per week for months, you may want to schedule

two to three half-day meetings). Steering committees often need to meet monthly or at least quarterly.

8 How? Establish expectations for effective meeting roles and processes, ground rules and communication processes. If the team is expected to report to the sponsor or other teams, be clear about how and how often they should do this. Discuss any assumptions about frameworks, assessments, tools, research and processes you expect that they use, as well as any other resources they may employ.

Team review agenda

When to use. After completing any project, the project team or task force should conduct a project review to distil their learning and verify completion of project goals. The insights from this review should be widely shared to promote organizational learning.

How to prepare. You can use the following agenda in Table 8.4 to conduct such a review. Send this out with your invitation to the team.

How to conduct. Lead the team through each of the following agenda items:

1 Goals: review the original goals and expectations for the project.
2 Successes and problems: compare the goals/expectations with the results/outcomes of the project. Sometimes this is framed as 'proud' and 'sorry'. What are you most proud about? What do you wish might have been different? If desired, take time to recognize each team member, thanking each person for their contribution and asking each person how he or she grew by participating on the project.
3 Lessons: distil the lessons from this experience in two areas:
   • content – what you learned from the focus of the project;
   • process – what you learned about working as a team.
4 Recommendations: develop specific recommendations for management and other teams and discuss how to institutionalize them:
   • future sustainability projects;
   • improvements to processes for managing teams and projects.

Table 8.4 *Team review worksheet*

Team:	Date of review:
Goal(s):	Results:
Successes:	Problems:
Lessons:	Recommendations:

Critical incident analysis

When to use. It's important for organizations to learn from their experience. This post mortem helps to get the most learning out of critical or noteworthy incidences. Conduct it as soon after the event as possible before memories fade. Note that if the outcome was negative, it can be very important to use a neutral facilitator.

How to prepare. Gather any outcome data relevant to the incident being studied so that the group can make data-based assessments and plans.

How to conduct this activity. Begin by establishing a set of ground rules. Then follow the steps below.

Ground rules. Explain the assumptions behind a critical incident analysis, including the following:

- Assume positive intent. Don't attribute nefarious intentions behind people's actions. Assume that everyone is operating with goodwill unless proven otherwise.
- Speak for yourself. Tell the truth as you see it, describing behaviours, emotions and results.
- Focus on the system. The system in which we operate is often a powerful predictor of behaviour. Look for the root causes.
- Focus on understanding and learning. This is not about affixing blame or kudos. It's about understanding what led to the outcome, positive or negative, so that the organization can become increasingly more effective.

Then review the incident following these steps:

1 Chronology: map out what happened when. Let each person involved speak uninterrupted, adding detail to the map.
2 Analysis: compare this chronology and results to desired outcomes. Depending upon your purpose, this might involve analysing it against corporate values, customer requirements, a sustainability framework or corporate goals. Talk about what contributed to the outcome. It can help to organize the conversation into 'helping forces' and 'hindering forces'.
3 Future: distil the lessons learned for the future. If a similar situation comes up, what would bolster the helping forces and mitigate the hindering forces?
4 Institutionalization: decide how best to integrate the lessons learned within the standard operating practices of the organization.

NOTE

1 A few portions of this chapter were excerpted from a yet-unpublished manual we wrote for Idaho GEM*Stars*, a voluntary environmental recognition programme.

Informing and Involving Employees

CONCEPTS AND CASE EXAMPLES

Given how busy people are, you'll want a comprehensive communication plan to keep sustainability at the forefront of people's minds. Not only will a concerted communication effort maintain the momentum of your sustainability effort, it will help all stakeholders to understand the issues and frameworks related to sustainability and enable employees to see opportunities to reduce waste, costs and impacts, as well as discover innovations. Communicating with and training all employees also gives them a shared mental model, a way of organizing and talking about the issues, and facilitates cooperation across organizational boundaries. Helping people to understand the concepts and its application to an organization has also been shown to be a powerful motivator. Employees feel good about working for a company that wants to ensure a desirable future for their children.

In this chapter, we'll share tips for:

- sharing information;
- involving employees;
- training employees.

We'll also explore some of the special challenges associated with teaching and communicating about sustainability.

Sharing information

Communication is crucial to any organizational change effort. At the beginning, you have to let employees know what you are pursuing and why. This inevitably unleashes a flood of questions, confusions and concerns, which, in turn, leads to a need for more communication. As your sustainability effort progresses, you have to maintain a sense of momentum by letting people know what you are doing and accomplishing. If you forget to remind everyone that your organization is committed to sustainability, organizational inertia will set in; people will forget about it and go back to the old way of doing things. The risks of not communicating well are worse than just people being in the dark. You risk feeding the flavour-of-the-month cynicism, which is all too common in organizations. You want your communication to be inspiring and inviting as more and more employees get excited about contributing. You need your communication to touch all critical parties often enough to keep sustainability alive in their minds. This only happens with careful planning and disciplined execution.

Your sustainability plan provides the starting place for thinking about your communication efforts. Scan your plan to identify the key audiences with whom you will want to communicate. Examine your project ideas for places to involve and inform employees. Be sure to let people know not only what the organization is doing, but how they can contribute and how much progress you are making as you go along.

Consider the best media for your communication with each stakeholder group. Use a combination of print, email, displays and other tools. Leverage the media you already use. If you already have an organizational newsletter, for example, consider making updates on your sustainability efforts a regular feature so that people will get used to watching for sustainability news. If you don't have a newsletter, perhaps you could begin a routine of regular e-blasts to keep your lines of communication open. Another useful venue for communication is any regularly occurring meeting. Staff meetings, management meetings, safety meetings all could be used to deliver updates on the effort. In addition to providing a viable medium for delivering information, talking about sustainability during a regular meeting sends the message that it is a business issue and has the constant attention of leadership.

Use other existing events to get the sustainability message out. Informal events, such as holiday parties, can be used to share information or highlight aspects of sustainability by serving local and in-season produce and offering sustainable gifts. You can also use your sustainability efforts to create new events. Many organizations hold sustainability or green fairs, inviting vendors of green products to display their wares and local government and non-profit groups to share educational resources. Or offer study groups (a good example are the discussion courses offered through the Northwest Earth Institute) or brown bag sessions that feature presenters from other organizations.

In addition to these venues, consider creating a 'go-to source' where people can seek out information in between your updates. A web page on your organization's site is a logical mechanism for providing ongoing and up-to-date information. It is also a good mechanism for storing archived materials, such as past years' sustainability reports or even shared files to which people can contribute. You may also want to create a hotline or suggestion system for people to share their concerns and ideas.

As you prepare your written and oral messages, keep these considerations in mind:

- Tailor the content and language to the audience. We are not implying that you tell different stories to different people. Honesty, clarity and integrity are key! But do consider the interests, concerns, biases and knowledge of your various audiences. Determine which terms will resonate with employees and which will put them off. Share stories and examples that will be meaningful and inspirational. Use easy-to-understand language and avoid terms that might be confusing or considered buzzwords. We often talk about the *rules* of The Natural Step, for example, instead of using the less friendly term *system conditions*.
- Share many inspiring examples of what other organizations have done. At least some of the examples should touch on relevant opportunities that your organization may have; but be careful not to pick situations that are too close to your own or you'll find that people will interpret your examples as directives or throw up objections such as: 'That won't work here because …'.
- Remember: not everyone is as concerned about the environment or social justice as you are. So, keep your message factual. Focus on the opportunities rather than the scary trends. Don't push people too hard or you'll push them away.

BOX 9.1 STOEL RIVES LLP GENERATES EXCITEMENT

Stoel Rives, a law firm with 11 offices throughout the western US as well as in Minneapolis, Minnesota, has had a long history of environmental awareness beginning in the 1980s. During the last year or two, however, it has embraced sustainability and taken both its internal practices and external reputation to another level. The sustainability team spent nearly a year drafting a sustainability initiative and plan they called 'Go Green', quietly making changes in its internal practices. Although successful, it wanted to increase the level of awareness and involvement among employees and held a major event in April 2008. It was the first time the firm had ever held a meeting for all staff and attorneys in all of the offices. Using video conferencing technology, it convened nearly every one of the 850 employees for a presentation by the managing partner and the firm's 'Go Green' sustainability team. The managing partner spoke about the importance of sustainability to the firm's practice areas, its reputation in the market and its ability to recruit new talent. The sustainability team educated the staff on several sustainability-related efforts, including energy savings. Phil Moran, the firm's administrative services manager, noticed that the meeting created a palpable change in office energy and facilitated the successful adoption of many of its latest initiatives (e.g. removal of desk-side waste baskets and the introduction of an office composting bin). There is a wider appreciation for what the firm is doing. Phil is convinced that their work has paid bonuses in morale and in the firm's recruiting efforts. Next up: a bicycling commute competition among the 11 offices.

Box 9.2 TriMet: Letting the data speak for itself

Sometimes the data speaks for itself. TriMet, the transit authority for Portland, Oregon, during one month of high electricity use at its rail facility, posted the electricity bill in the elevator, without entreaties or comment. When employees saw how much they spent on energy, they modified their behaviour. Their electricity bill dropped by 20 per cent the next month! It turns out that just providing this feedback can sometimes be enough to get people to take action.

Eliciting input and participation

In addition to delivering information to people, you will want to create mechanisms for them to get involved. Before you communicate with or train employees, ensure that you have systems in place to manage the inevitable ideas that will ensue. We've seen too many organizations get ahead of themselves. More than one organization has trained all of its employees on sustainability, getting them excited about what can be done, but then had no mechanism for them to submit ideas or any system in place for reviewing and responding to their input. At the very least, create (or resurrect) an employee suggestion process. Make sure that people know how, when and what they should contribute. Explain the process for evaluating and responding to suggestions, as well as the process for determining which get implemented. Some of the considerations you should take into account include:

- how to make the system easy to use;
- how the ideas will be evaluated and how quickly they should be responded to;
- the criteria for evaluating the ideas;
- any recognition/rewards for the ideas that are implemented.

By the way, the results of this process make natural fodder for the news updates described above!

The team structure described in Chapter 8 is another way to manage two-way communications with staff. Make sure that employees know about the opportunities to join teams. Determine if you will accept all volunteers or if there are certain criteria that members need to meet in order to participate. In order to facilitate the communication among and between teams, coordinate their operating practices. Design a common reporting format and schedule, for example, so that the coordinators of the initiative have a manageable way to stay on top of what is going on. These reports can be fed into the steering committee or to the sustainability director to make for a smooth system for managing the effort.

BOX 9.3 NW NATURAL PROVIDES MANY WAYS FOR EMPLOYEES TO BE INVOLVED

NW Natural, a gas utility in Portland, Oregon, developed a number of structures to involve employees. In addition to the small Environmental Policy and Sustainability Department, it also created a couple of other teams. SustainNet is what is known in the organizational development field as a community of practice. It's an informal group that is officially sanctioned by management but not directed by management. SustainNet was a place for people with a passion for sustainability to meet, share ideas and explore ideas for expanding sustainability in the organization. NW Natural also identified Mavens and Mentors, people in individual departments who could provide a liaison with the organization. After a while, the firm decided that it also needed a steering committee to advise the Environmental Policy and Sustainability Department staff. Since the department doesn't have position authority over all other departments, the steering committee adds a mechanism involving the departments in decisions that will affect them. All together, these structures give a significant percentage of employees a formal role in supporting sustainability.

Training on sustainability

Training is more complex than just sharing information. Training implies that you verify that people learned something and can do something new as a result of the training. It's unrealistic, for example, to expect that a one-hour presentation on The Natural Step framework will be adequate to change behaviour. There's a lot more to training than telling!

We know from many years of research that teaching adults involves leveraging what they already know and sometimes 'unlearning' concepts or habits that are no longer useful. Adults are motivated to learn when they have a compelling reason to need or use the information. They worry about looking stupid and don't want to be embarrassed; they don't like being tested. So when you design training, keep these concepts in mind:

- Explain up front why your employees need to learn what you are covering, and why it's important to your business and to them personally.
- Don't give them more than they can absorb at one time. Do just-in-time training so that they get the skills they need when they need them. During any training session, change what you're doing at least every 20 minutes to maintain attention. You might give a 15-minute presentation, engage them in a discussion about it, and then give them an exercise to apply the concepts.

- Help your employees link what you are teaching to things they already know. Involve them in the training by asking many questions so that they can show off what they know and stay engaged.
- Provide learning activities that give you feedback about how much they are learning but are less threatening than tests. Exercises and instructional games can often accomplish this (see Galea, 2004, 2007, for sample exercises). Provide specific opportunities to apply what they have learned, as well, so that they can integrate the content within their everyday work.
- Give them a job aid: something that will help them remember and use the information. This may be a worksheet, a poster, a binder of materials, a step-by-step process, etc.
- You may want to call your sessions something other than training because people often associate training with artificial environments from which they return to the real world. Instead, consider embedding training within a task force meeting, briefing, working session, team meeting, etc. Find language that communicates that what you are covering relates directly to the work they should be doing.

BOX 9.4 COLLINS COMPANY: PROVIDING JOB AIDS TO HELP EMPLOYEES INTEGRATE SUSTAINABILITY

The wood products company, Collins, developed several job aids to ensure that people were thinking about sustainability when they made major purchases as well as when they began projects. They didn't want sustainability to be something extra that people did; instead, it was just an extra filter that people use when they make decisions. Here are two of their tools.

EXPENDITURE REQUISITION CHECKLIST

PROJECT_____

1   Will this project increase or decrease energy usage (i.e. electricity/steam) in comparison to the existing system?   Explain!
2   Will this project require the use of chemicals? **Y/N**
    If yes, what type of chemicals, more or less than currently used, and how much per week, per month, per year?
3   Will this project require the use of consumable supplies (i.e. packaging)? **Y/N**
    If yes, explain.
4   Will this project affect air emissions, point source or fugitive, indoor or outdoor? **Y/N**
    If yes, can it be measured? **Y/N**
    If yes, explain.

5   Will this project require the use of water in any way? **Y/N**
    If yes, explain.
6   Will this project create or increase any form of waste? **Y/N**
    If yes, explain.
7   How will this project impact the 3 Rs, (reduce, reuse and recycle)? Whether you answer
    yes or no, make sure you address them in the expenditure requisition (ER) narrative.
8   Will this project affect the use of *man-made* chemicals and compounds? **Y/N**
    If yes, explain.
9   Will this project increase our use of materials extracted from the
    Earth's crust (i.e. metals)? **Y/N**
    If yes, explain.
10 Can construction be altered to minimize our use of natural resources,
    minimize waste material and maximize the use of recycled materials? **Y/N**
    Please explain.
11 Will this project result in an increase in board production? **Y/N**
    If yes, explain.

KLAMATH FALLS (SUSTAINABILITY PROJECT) EVALUATION SUMMARY AND RECOMMENDATION

PROJECT:_____

Does this project: (circle one)
Reduce dependence upon fossil fuels and mining?   Yes/Neutral/No
Reduce dependence upon compounds produced by society
    that can accumulate in nature?   Yes/Neutral/No
Reduce dependence upon activities that intrude on productive parts of
    nature (e.g. long road transports): paving over green surfaces?   Yes/Neutral/No
Increase the efficiency with which resources are used?   Yes/Neutral/No
This project is approved/not approved by the JTS team.
Date:_____

Special challenges regarding the topic of sustainability[1]

Teaching sustainability in business presents a number of unique challenges. The task is
more complex than a typical corporate change effort because the goals are arguably more
complex: to change how people see the world, to convince them that they can make a
difference to a global problem and to give them tools that they can use in their daily lives.

You may have to manage high expectations because employees may become impatient with the pace of corporate change when they understand the magnitude of the problem. They must also plan the implementation so that the organization's profitability is maintained while it researches and tries to develop new methods. The leaders of the organization must be able to envision the end game so that they do not invest in dead-end technologies. Few of us are adept at thinking at the scale and timeframes required for sustainability.

. Further complicating the process, people often become confused and overwhelmed by the honest and not-so-honest debate that swirls around many environmental issues. It's also frequently difficult for people to grasp an abstract concept such as sustainability and to adopt the necessary systems perspective of business practices. Given that sustainability is still a new movement, you'll have to overcome the inertia of a business community that is just now waking up to the strategic importance of sustainability.

We've uncovered strategies that work (and have abandoned some that don't) as we have worked with organizations to overcome these obstacles. In Table 9.1, we list common learning outcomes and suggest exercises that accomplish these objectives. Some of the exercises have already been presented in earlier chapters but are also useful in training sessions. We have added a couple of easy exercises at the end of this chapter and have also provided resources where you can obtain instructions for other exercises as well.

Tips

- Base your training and communication plan on stakeholders' needs. Make sure that the information you give them is appropriate to their situation, familiarity with the issues and points of view.
- Avoid 'spray-and-pray' training. Some organizations like to start by training all employees on sustainability. However, rarely are these organizations ready to launch sustainability simultaneously across the organization. One company found itself two years later with hundreds of employee suggestions that hadn't been vetted or addressed. This is a major mistake. Instead, do just-in-time training. Train groups of people as they are likely to need it, and slowly, over time, deepen their knowledge.
- Use easily understood demonstrations, analogies and examples to help people understand any scientific principles. For example, you can refer to perfume to explain entropy: how everything spreads. If you want to explain tolerances and thresholds, many people are aware that different houseplants demonstrate wide variances in drought tolerance.
- Allow enough time to get to what people can do; don't just leave people overwhelmed with the sad state of the world. Take time to let them think of tangible actions that they can take right away.

Table 9.1 *Learning strategies and recommended exercises*

Learning outcome	Suggested exercises
Understanding the concepts and science behind sustainability and getting the passion	*Sustainability business simulation.* We created a business simulation that shows people how to do an impact assessment and derive common practices to become more sustainable. This simulation has a strong industrial ecology component. Industries represented include food processing, medical, small manufacturing and high-tech. The full instructions and materials are published in *Teaching Business Sustainability* (Galea, 2007).
	The Natural Step card activity. This exercise helps to anchor the science and systems conditions associated with The Natural Step framework. The materials are published in *Teaching Business Sustainability* (Galea, 2007).
	Worldwide trend cards. This exercise gets people to examine troublesome trends (see Chapter 2).
	Everyday choices exercise. This exercise helps people to apply a framework such as The Natural Step in everyday situations in order to make more sustainable decisions. Instructions are included at the end of this chapter.
What it means to your job	*Impact assessment.* Conduct an impact assessment at the job or workgroup level using the process we presented in Chapter 4.
	SCORE™. Implement the SCORE™ assessment – see a version in *The Business Guide to Sustainability* (Hitchcock and Willard, 2006) and go to www.axisperformance.com for licensed assessors.
Dealing with the threat reaction; dealing with emotional defences	*Threats and opportunities.* Use this exercise to build confidence that your organization can find business opportunities, even if its current business model is clearly unsustainable. This exercise can also help people to understand the business case for pursuing sustainability (see instructions in Chapter 2).
	Site visits and speakers. Take employees on visits to other organizations; invite guest speakers; share case studies. As much as possible, link people with near-peers: people who are a lot like them and do similar work.
	Joanna Macy has several creative exercises for helping people with the emotional transition (see Macy, 1998).
Thinking creatively – developing systems thinking; adopting new mental models	*Sustainability business simulation.* See description above.
	Backcasting. Envisioning your organization in a fully sustainable state is a powerful visioning exercise (see Chapter 3).
	New Business Model. This activity helps people to get beyond the quick wins in order to understand how they can move towards a fully sustainable state (see Chapter 3).

- Be careful not to let the discussion devolve into blaming. Pointing fingers and talking about what people *should do* will raise defensiveness. Sustainability shouldn't be about not having what we want; it should be about having what we want *sustainably.*
- You, the instructor, don't have to be the expert. If you don't know the answer to a question, see if anyone else in the room does or offer to research it.
- Build basic concepts into your orientation. Too many organizations do an initial blitz of training and then forget that turnover happens. After a few years, a significant percentage of the employees may not have received the initial training. So, make sure every new employee gets the basics in their orientation.

RESOURCES

Books and articles

- Galea, C. (ed) (2004) *Teaching Business Sustainability, Volume 1: From Theory to Practice,* Greenleaf Publishing, Sheffield, UK
- Galea, C. (ed) (2007) Teaching Business Sustainability, Volume 2: Cases, Simulations and Experiential Approaches, Greenleaf Publishing, Sheffield, UK
- Macy, J. (1998) *Coming Back to Life,* New Society Publisher, Gabriola Island, BC, Canada;
- Hitchcock, D. (1988) 'Building instructional games', *TRAINING Magazine,* March, pp33–39.

Videos and DVDs

Check out the fabulous film libraries at Public Broadcasting (www.shoppbs.org) and the BBC (in the UK: www.bbc.co.uk; in the US: www.bbcamericashop.com/video). For short clips, try YouTube.com.
  Some specific videos we've liked include:

- *Crude Impact* (about the impacts of oil production), www.crudeimpact.com;
- *Ella Baker Center: The First 10 Years* (Van Jones; relates to social justice and green jobs), http://ellabakercenter.org;
- *The Next Industrial Revolution* (Bill McDonough; relates to cradle-to-cradle design in buildings and manufacturing), www.thenextindustrialrevolution.org;
- *The Power of Community: How Cuba Survived Peak Oil* (about peak oil), www.powerofcommunity.org.

METHODS AND INSTRUCTIONS

In this section, we explain six activities or processes that are helpful in developing training and communication plans and events.

Communication plan

When to use. Always! Make sure that you are clear about how, when and what you will communicate to your stakeholders to keep your effort moving forward.

How to prepare. We recommend making this part of your planning process. Once you have your sustainability plan drafted, use it to determine who, how and when you need to communicate.

How to conduct this activity:

1   List the stakeholders along the top row and the timeframes along the left side.
2   Plug in the activities you already have planned. These may include monthly steering committee meetings, reports at regular board meetings or training events.
3   For each stakeholder group, set a goal for how many times you should communicate with them about sustainability. For boards and customers, this might be only once a year; but for employees it should be much more frequent.
4   Brainstorm ways to 'touch' every stakeholder group. Be creative! You can post informational signs on restroom doors, send out short sustainability factoids to an email list or plan a Green Fair. A partially completed sample form is provided in Table 9.3. Make it fun, quirky, inspiring, practical, and perhaps even controversial.

Table 9.2 *Overview of methods for involving employees*

Process	When to use
Communication plan	This is a good place to start organizing your communication effort.
Training plan	A comprehensive approach to preparing the whole organization for change.
Lesson plan	When you need to develop training.
Impact assessment	This will help people to understand how sustainability applies to their individual jobs.
Everyday choices	This quick activity is a fun way for people to test their knowledge of the principles of sustainability.
Personal sustainability assessment	This activity helps people to make commitments to personal change.

Table 9.3 Sample communication plan

	Board	Top management	Sustainability steering committee	Sustainability task forces	Professional employees (with access to email)	Field employees (w/o email)	Customers	Suppliers	Legislators
Frequency goal	1 year	2 years	12 years	Monthly while in existence	12 years	6 years	1 year	4 years	2 years
January	Annual sustainability report	Annual sustainability report			Tip in newsletter: energy conservation	Tip in newsletter: energy conservation			
February					Luncheon speaker: nature-scaping presentation				
March					Tip: waste reduction	Tip: waste reduction			
April					Luncheon speaker: climate change				
May					Green Fair	Green Fair	Green Fair	Green Fair	
June		Energy conservation challenge							
July		Semi-annual progress report							
August		Energy conservation challenge	Energy conservation challenge	Energy conservation challenge	Energy conservation challenge	Energy conservation challenge		Energy conservation challenge	

Training plan

When to use. If your organization and your sustainability effort are large enough, you will want to develop a thoughtful approach to ensuring that everyone is trained in the key concepts and activities of the effort.

How to prepare. Let your implementation plan be your guide. Look at your schedule and your project ideas and let them suggest what people will need to know and when they will need to know it.

How to conduct this activity. Use the form in Table 9.4 during one of your planning meetings. Start with your communication plan to see if any of the stakeholders need training and then add any special populations or departments within your organization. For each stakeholder ask the following:

*   What do we want them to be able to *do* that they are not doing now (skills)?
*   What will they need to know in order to demonstrate the behaviour you identified above. Or should they be able to explain to others in their departments (knowledge)?
*   What materials or affiliations will help them to obtain this new knowledge and apply their new skills (resources and affiliations)?

Lesson plan

When to use. When you want to design a training event tailored to your organization's particular needs.

How to prepare. Refer to your training plan for the specific learning objectives (skills and knowledge) that the participants are to achieve. Always begin with a clear end in mind. Ask: 'What should the participants be able to *do* after this event?' This will help you to design clear, focused and relevant training.

How to conduct this activity. Let the template in Table 9.5 be your guide for thinking through all the components critical to a learning event. As you lay out this plan, remember to allow time for breaks and questions/discussions.

Everyday choices

When to use. This is a general activity you can use to introduce the concepts of sustainability. It works well with adults as well as school-age children because it deals with everyday decisions.

How to prepare. Lay out the examples listed below on cards, supplemented with pictures cut from magazines. We encourage you to make up your own cards with different

Table 9.4 *Sample training plan*

Stakeholder group	Everyone	Top management	Sustainability director and steering committee	Design engineers	Facilities	Purchasing
Knowledge	The Natural Step system conditions	Global Reporting Initiative guidelines Carbon Disclosure Project	Organizational change concepts	Design for environment principles	LEED for Existing Buildings	Green purchasing concepts
Skills	Impact assessment	Communicate the business case	Sustainability planning process	Life-cycle assessments	Greenhouse gas inventory Waste inventory Energy management	Life-cycle costing
Resources and affiliation		World Business Council on Sustainability	International Society of Sustainability Professionals	American Center for Life Cycle Assessment	US Green Building Council	Sustainable Purchasing Network

everyday decisions. You could, for example, add cards for work-related decisions. Leave off the codes that we have provided which give the answers (+, –).

How to conduct this activity. Put the class into small groups and give each group a card. Ask them to analyse the choices that they are given: which is the best and worst, based on The Natural Step or other framework. Give them a few minutes to discuss and then have some or all groups report their answers and rationale. We have put a plus sign (+) next to the best and a minus sign (–) next to the worst option, based on our assumptions, our location in the Pacific Northwest and the best information we could obtain (based on your assumptions or geographic location, different answers might be the best choices).

How to debrief. Let people report on their choices. Take time to emphasize that if you really love the 'worst choice' (e.g. golf or beef), then think about how to get that sustainably. How could you create a more sustainable golf course or cattle farm?

Table 9.5 *Sample lesson plan*

Objective	Primary learning points	Method/Audio/Visual	Who	Time
Introduce the session	Welcome participants and explain the importance of the session, how it relates to other training and what expectations there are after the training.	Informal presentation	Plant manager	5 minutes
	Explain the learning objectives.	Wall chart	Instructor	2 minutes
	Let participants introduce themselves.	Give name, department and something they've done related to sustainability at home or work.	Instructor	20 minutes
1 Explain why pursuing sustainability is important to the business.	Create list of social, economic and environmental challenges faced by the company.	Brainstorm with the whole class on the flipchart.	Instructor	10 minutes
	Explore how they interrelate.	Interactive lecture	Instructor	5 minutes
	Activity: create a short 'elevator speech' to explain why our company is pursuing sustainability.	Small group exercise	Table groups	10 minutes
	Activity: Pick the winner.	Have each group say their elevator speech, comparing two at a time. Start with two and have the audience vote on the better one. Then add another and vote again.	Instructor led	30 minutes
2 Explain the four system conditions and the science behind them.				

- You are at the grocery store to buy juice …
  - Buy frozen juice (–).
  - Buy fruit and make your own juice (+).
  - Buy fruit juice – not from concentrate.

- You are landscaping part of your yard …
  - Plant a western red cedar tree (+ for Pacific Northwest; replace with a native tree in your area).
  - Plant grass (–).
  - Plant a tulip tree.

- You are choosing a sport for exercise …
  - Play golf (–).
  - Play baseball.
  - Do snow shoeing (+) (if snow shoeing is possible nearby).

- Your family is deciding on a holiday …
  - Go on a canoe trip in the Cascades (+ for Pacific Northwest).
  - Fly to Hawaii.
  - Take a cruise (–).

- You are buying cleaning products …
  - Buy Orange Plus.
  - Buy Lysol in an aerosol can (–).
  - Buy 409 in a spray bottle.
  - Use baking soda and vinegar (+).

- You are thirsty …
  - Drink bottled water.
  - Grab a soft drink (–).
  - Get water from tap (+).

- You are choosing personal care products …
  - Buy Tom's of Maine.
  - Buy Dry Idea.
  - Buy deodorant stone (+).

- You are picking what to eat at a restaurant …
  - Order beef: a steak or hamburger (–).

- Order chicken.
- Order spaghetti with marinara sauce (+).

- You are choosing a hobby ...
  - Get into digital photography (+)
  - Hike/backpack.
  - Go fishing in motorized boats (–).

- You're at the checkout counter at the grocery store ...
  - Ask for paper bags.
  - Ask for plastic bags (–).
  - Bring your own canvas bags (+).

- You want breakfast ...
  - Eat oatmeal (+).
  - Eat cold cereal.
  - Eat a frozen waffle (–).

Impact assessment

Use the 'High-level impact assessment' from Chapter 4 at the workgroup or individual level. This helps to bring sustainability down to their level and identifies things that they can do.

Personal sustainability assessment

When to use. This is another general activity that encourages people to make personal commitments to change.

How to prepare. Provide copies of the worksheets below (see Table 9.6).

How to conduct this activity. Give each person a copy of the assessment. Either have participants complete the assessment in class or encourage them to take it home and go through it with their families. Ask each person to pick a short-term item for improvement (something they can affect right away) and a long-term one (which they might take into account the next time, for example, they have to purchase a durable good):

1   Read through the assessment and circle the answers that most accurately reflect your household's situation. A couple of the items may require that you track things for a week (e.g. waste) or do a little figuring (e.g. living space.) It's best to gather real data; but use estimates if you need to.

Table 9.6 *Personal sustainability assessment*

	Habits:			
Household activity	*Best practice*	*Good work*	*Could be improved*	*Hard on the Earth*
Transportation: do you most often ...	Bike/walk	Take public transportation	Carpool	Drive alone
Diet: do you most often eat meals that ...	Are vegetarian from organic and/or local sources	Include fish or chicken from certified sources and only occasionally include produce from more than 500 miles away	Include pork, non-certified fish and poultry	Include beef and regularly include produce from more than 1500 miles away
Household waste: do you	Recycle and compost everything possible	Recycle most things	Recycle only what you get paid for (e.g. 5 cent returns on bottles)	Put everything in the garbage
Waste: weigh your garbage after one week. Is it ...	Less than 0.25lbs per person	Between 0.25 to 1lb per person	Between 1 to 2lbs per person	> 2lbs per person
Bathing: do you usually ...	Take showers that last less than 5 minutes with a low-flow shower head	Take showers that last 5 to 8 minutes with a low-flow shower head	Take showers that last more than 8 minutes	Take baths instead of showers most of the time
Purchases: do you ...	Use everything until you wear it out, repair it or give it away to others; buy in bulk; consider the packaging in your purchase decision	Repair what is cost effective; donate what you don't need	Use shopping as a form of recreation, often buying things you don't need	Buy the latest version (e.g. computer, sound system, etc.) or remodel even though your existing possessions are still in good shape

Table 9.6 *Personal sustainability assessment* (Cont'd)

House:				
Household activity	*Best practice*	*Good work*	*Could be improved*	*Hard on the Earth*
Square footage: divide the living space in your house (in square feet) by the number in your household. Is your square feet per person …	Less than 500 square feet	500 to 1000 square feet	1000 to 1500 square feet	Over 1500 square feet
Appliances: how many of your appliances are energy and water efficient (refrigerator, washing machine, dish washer, furnace, etc.)?	All	75%	50%	25% or less
Lighting: how many of the lights you use for more than two hours a day are energy-efficient fluorescents or light-emitting diodes (LEDs)?	All	75%	50%	25% or less
Heat/cooling: do you set your thermostat to …	66°F (19°C) or less; don't use air conditioning	68°F (20°C) or less; don't use air conditioning	70°F (21°C) or less; don't use air conditioning	71°F (22°C) or more; use air conditioning

Table 9.6 *Personal sustainability assessment* (Cont'd)

House:				
Household activity	*Best practice*	*Good work*	*Could be improved*	*Hard on the Earth*
Weatherization: how well insulated is your house (consider windows, caulking, insulation, etc.)? Is your house ...	Tight as a drum (but properly ventilated as with an energy-recovery ventilation system)	Pretty tight	Has a few noticeable drafts/leaks	Is well below current codes
Energy: where does your energy come from? Do you ...	Buy 100% green power and/or generate power from solar or other systems	Buy at least 50% green power and use passive solar heating/cooling	Buy less than 50% green power but use energy wisely	Buy no green power and use energy wastefully
Outdoors:				
Landscaping: when you landscape your yard, do you ...	Choose all native plants and minimize lawn	Choose plants that attract wildlife (not all native plants)	Have a lot of lawn; most shrubs and trees are non-native	Have mostly lawn and some invasive non-native plants
Maintenance: do you ...	Never use synthetic pesticides/herbicides	Rarely use pesticides/herbicides	Sometimes use pesticides/herbicides	Frequently use pesticides/herbicides
Watering: do you ...	Never water the lawn; plant drought-resistant plants; use a rainwater collection system	Water shrubs and flowers only after a long dry spell	Water shrubs and flowers regularly	Water lawn regularly

2   Look at the items that you circled which are further to the right. These represent opportunities to become more sustainable. Some items might be easy to do right away (e.g. replace lights with compact fluorescent bulbs or walk to the store more often) and others might factor into future decisions (e.g. how much living space you really need or the efficiency of your appliances). Find one item that you're willing to improve and make a commitment.

3   Review the assessment in another month, acknowledge your progress and see if there's another improvement that you might be able to build into your habits.

NOTE

1   This section is adapted from Galea (2004).

References

CHAPTER 1

Anderson, L. A. and Anderson, D. (2001) *The Change Leader's Roadmap*, Jossey-Bass/Pfeiffer, San Francisco, CA

AtKisson, A. (2008) *The ISIS Agreement*, Earthscan, London

Axelrod, D. (2007) *How to Get People to Care About What You Find Important*, www.everyday engagement.com

Blackburn, W. R. (2008) *The Sustainability Handbook*, Earthscan, London

Doppelt, B. (2003) *Leading Change toward Sustainability*, Greenleaf Publishing, Sheffield, UK

Epstein, M. (2008) *Making Sustainability Work: Best Practices in Managing and Measuring Corporate Social, Environmental and Economic Impacts*, Greenleaf Publishing, Sheffield, UK

Hitchcock, D. and Willard, M. (2006) *The Business Guide to Sustainability*, Earthscan, London

Maurer, R. (1996) Beyond the Wall of Resistance, Bard Books, Austin, TX

Meadows, D. H. (1997) 'Places to intervene in a system: in increasing order of effectiveness', *Whole Earth*, Winter

Nattrass, B. and Altomare, M. (2002) *Dancing with the Tiger*, New Society Publishers, Gabriola Island, BC, Canada

Senge, P. M., Kleiner, A., Roberts, C. and Roth, G. (1999) *The Dance of Change: The Challenges to Sustaining Momentum in Learning Organizations*, Doubleday, New York

CHAPTER 2

Centers for Disease Control and Prevention (2003) *Second National Report on Human Exposure to Environmental Chemicals*, Centers for Disease Control and Prevention

Heath, C. and Heath, D. (2007) *Made to Stick: Why Some Ideas Survive and Others Die*, Random House, New York

IPCC (Intergovernmental Panel on Climate Change) (2007) *Climate Change 2007: Synthesis Report – Summary for Policy Makers*, An Assessment of the Intergovernmental Panel on Climate Change, Fourth Assessment Report (AR4), IPCC Plenary XXVII, Valencia, Spain, 12–17 November 2007

MA (Millennium Assessment) (2005) Millennium Assessment Reports, available for download at www.millenniumassessment.org

Steingraber, S. (2001) *Having Faith: An Ecologist's Journey to Motherhood*, Perseus Publishing, Cambridge, MA

Wackernagel, M. (2000) *Sharing Nature's Interest: Ecological Footprints as an Indicator of Sustainability*, Earthscan, London

Willard, B. (2002) *The Sustainability Advantage: Seven Business Case Benefits of a Triple Bottom Line*, New Society Publishers, Gabriola Island, BC, Canada

WRI (World Resources Institute) (no date) 'Falling frontiers', www.wri.org/publication/content/8276, accessed 26 August 2008

CHAPTER 3

Anielski, M. (2007) *The Economics of Happiness: Building Genuine Wealth*, New Society Publishers, Gabriola Island, BC, Canada

Cook, D. (2004) *The Natural Step: Towards a Sustainable Society*, Green Books, Bristol, UK

Edwards, A. R. (2005) *The Sustainability Revolution: Portrait of a Paradigm Shift*, New Society Publishers, Gabriola Island, BC, Canada

EPA (2007) 'State of the Environment (SoE) reporting frameworks', Environmental Protection Agency of South Australia, www.epa.sa.gov.au/soe_frame.html, accessed 26 August 2008

Gray, E. R. and Balmer, J. M. (2004) *Working Paper Series: The Sustainable Entrepreneur*, Working Paper No 04/14, March, www.bradford.ac.uk/acad/management/external/pdf/workingpapers/2004/Booklet_04-14.pdf

Hallsmith, G. (2003) *The Key to Sustainable Cities: Meeting Human Needs, Transforming Community Systems*, New Society Publishers, Gabriola Island, BC, Canada

Hitchcock, D. and Willard, M. (2006) *The Business Guide to Sustainability*, Earthscan, London

Robert, K. H., Schmidt-Blee, B., Aloisi de Larderel, J., Basile, G., Jansen, J. L., Keuhr, R., Price Thomas, P., Suzuki, M., Hawken, P. and Wackernagel, M. (2002) 'Strategic sustainable development: Selection, design and synergies of applied tools', *Journal of Cleaner Production*, vol 10, pp197–214

WCED (World Commission on Environment and Development) (1987) *Our Common Future, The Brundtland Report*, Oxford University Press, Oxford

CHAPTER 4

Duke Castle (2001) *A Sustainability Vision for the Automotive Services Industry: Using The Natural Step Framework to Develop a Plan Toward Sustainability for Automotive Mechanical and Collision Repair Shops*, Report prepared for Oregon Department of Environmental quality by Duke Castle of the Castle Group, Lake Oswego, Oregon, Funded by USEPA Region X Office Seattle, Washington Pollution Prevention Incentives for States Grant June 2001

US Environmental Protection Agency (no date) *Lean and Environment Toolkit*, version 1, www.epa.gov/lean/toolkit/LeanEnviroToolkit.pdf

CHAPTER 5

AXIS (2008) *SPaRK™: Sustainability Planning and Reporting Kit*, www.axisperformance.com

Bayon, R., Hawn, A. and Hamilton, K. (2007) *Voluntary Carbon Markets: An International Business Guide to What they Are and How they Work*, Earthscan, London

Corporate Register (2008) *Global Winners and Reporting Trends*, www.corporateregister.com

Hart, M. (2006) *Guide to Sustainable Community Indicators*, Sustainable Measures, Hartford, CT, www.sustainablemeasures.com

Kohn, Alfie (1986) *No Contest: The Case against Competition*, Houghton Mifflin, Boston, MA

Kohn, Alfie (1993) *Punished by Rewards: The Trouble with Gold Stars, Incentive Plans, A's, Praise, and Other Bribes*, Houghton Mifflin, Boston, MA

WRI (World Resources Institute) (2002) *Working 9 to 5 on Climate Change: An Office Guide*, December, available for download from www.wri.org/publication/working-9-5-climate-change-office-guide, accessed 26 August 2008

CHAPTER 6

Doppelt, B. (2003) *Leading Change toward Sustainability*, Greenleaf Publishing, Sheffield, UK

Epstein, M. (2008) *Making Sustainability Work: Best Practices in Managing and Measuring Corporate Social, Environmental and Economic Impacts*, Greenleaf Publishing, Sheffield, UK

Oregon Natural Step (2002) *Oregon Natural Step Network Tool Kit*, 'Ashforth Pacific Case Study', p2, www.ortns.org/documents/AshforthPacificupOct02.pdf, accessed 13 May 2008

CHAPTER 7

Hitchcock, D. and Atwood, D. (2002) *Developing Effective Systems for Managing Sustainability*, Sustainability Series™, AXIS Performance Advisors, Portland, OR

CHAPTER 8

AXIS Performance Advisors (2002) *Forming and Facilitating Sustainability Teams: Steering Committees to Task Forces*, www.axisperformance.com

Hackett, D. W. and Martin, C. (1993) *Crisp: Facilitation Skills for Team Leaders – Leading Organized Teams to Greater Productivity*, Crisp Fifty-Minute Series, Crisp Learning, Mississauga, Ontario, Canada

Justice, T. and Jamieson, D. (2006) *The Facilitator's Fieldbook*, second edition, HRD Press, New York, NY

Schwarz, R., Davidson, A., Carlson, P. and McKinney, S. (2005) *The Skilled Facilitator Fieldbook*, Jossey Bass, San Francisco, CA

CHAPTER 9

Galea, C. (ed) (2004) *Teaching Business Sustainability, Volume 1: From Theory to Practice*, Greenleaf Publishing, Sheffield, UK

Galea, C. (ed) (2007) *Teaching Business Sustainability, Volume 2: Cases, Simulations and Experiential Approaches*, Greenleaf Publishing, Sheffield, UK

Hitchcock, D. (1988) 'Building instructional games', *TRAINING Magazine*, March, pp33–39

Hitchcock, D. and Willard, M. (2006) *The Business Guide to Sustainability*, Earthscan, London

Macy, J. (1998) *Coming Back to Life*, New Society Publishers, Gabriola Island, BC, Canada

Appendix 1
Troubleshooting Tips

While having a solid, well-considered plan increases the likelihood that your implementation will be smooth and your success assured, we recognize that no plan is fool proof. Organizational change efforts are always unpredictable. We've added this appendix to share some of the common problems that we've seen organizations encounter along their path to sustainability and the strategies that have most often helped to resolve them.

Review the situations below. If you encounter one that is similar to problems that you are experiencing, then see if any of our suggestions fit your situation. We have organized the problems into four categories:

1   People are resistant to the concept of sustainability.
2   Sustainability is not seen as a strategic priority.
3   Employees don't see the relevance of sustainability in their jobs.
4   It takes extra effort to do the 'right thing'.

PEOPLE ARE RESISTANT TO THE CONCEPT OF SUSTAINABILITY

No matter how excited you are about sustainability, you will encounter resistance to it. The strategies that work best here are tied to the source of the resistance.

Provide information. Many people simply aren't well informed about the importance of sustainability to the future of civilization and their organization. Think about what information they need and who might be a credible source for that information.

Correct misinformation. Some sustainability-related issues have been publicly debated. In an attempt to show 'both sides of an issue', the news media likes to quote someone who is for the issue and someone against, without any recognition that one of those two parties may represent the consensus of most scientists in the world, while the other may be paid by special interest groups. This breeds misinformation and confusion on the part of the public. You may have to refute some of the 'facts' that people know. Again, think about what information they need and who might be a credible source for that information. Always preserve the other person's self esteem. Phrases such as: 'I thought that too until

I discovered ...' or 'I have heard that as well, but [a credible source] says ...' may help to correct their information without leaving them feeling censured.

Find the pay off. They may assume that doing the right thing for the environment is going to cost more (and sometimes it does). The trick here is to avoid per unit comparisons and look at total expenditures. You may be able to afford higher recycled-content paper if you start using both sides. Petroleum-based solvents may cost less per gallon; but because they may evaporate faster, they may cost more to use. It might cost you a little more to add green building features to your new construction project, but the energy savings might pay it back in a few years.

Unpack the baggage. Some people don't want to be associated with 'environmentalists'. Perhaps they've been offended by the tactics of certain environmental groups or their family has been negatively affected by environmental regulations that reduced employment in forestry, fishing or other extractive industries. In these situations, be careful not to 'push their buttons'. Avoid terms that are likely to link your efforts with what they might view as 'tree huggers'. Focus on the benefits to them and the organization.

Feed hope. For some people, the problems seem so insurmountable that they become despairing. Others deal with it through denial; they try not to think about it. One of the most important things you may need to do is to develop a sense of hopefulness. Rather than spending time spreading doom-and-gloom statistics, tell compelling stories about how other organizations have made a difference.

Empower and take bite-sized pieces. Sadly, many people in organizations feel powerless to change the system in which they work. They've come to accept (but resent) that 'there's nothing I can do'. In these situations, start with small steps that they can control. They may not be able to rewrite the corporate purchasing policy, but they may be able to ask their vendors about their environmental performance. When they need the approval of others, help them to build a strong case and, if necessary, do some behind-the-scenes lobbying to ensure their success.

SUSTAINABILITY IS NOT SEEN AS A STRATEGIC PRIORITY

Too often, sustainability initiatives are viewed predominately as something noble and nice to do for the planet. As long as this attitude prevails, it will always be perceived as something extra to do when there is spare time. It is leadership's responsibility to frame sustainability as the business issue that it is. Employees need to understand the strategic case for pursuing sustainability both in terms of the threats associated with ignoring it as well as the opportunities it presents for business improvements.

There are a number of ways, both subtle and explicit, in which leadership conveys the importance of sustainability to employees. Consider these strategies when launching your own effort.

Craft the business case. Translate sustainability trends into business issues and help employees to see how the organization will be affected by issues such as climate change, resource scarcity, consumer preferences and the like. Incorporate sustainability targets within your strategic plan. Draw the link between sustainability and previous initiatives to underscore the notion of continuous improvement and dispel the perception of fad hopping. Clarify why sustainability is the next natural step for your organization by linking it to past or existing efforts.

Hold managers accountable for results. Incorporate these expectations within plans, metrics and performance reviews. Expect managers to continuously address sustainability and regularly review progress on sustainability projects.

Incorporate sustainability within job descriptions. As long as employees believe that sustainability is something 'extra' to do, something on top of the already full plate of duties that they have and not part of what they will be evaluated on, it is unlikely that anything meaningful will change. When given the choice between doing what their bosses expect and what is perceived as an extra 'nice' task, sustainability will always float to the bottom of the To Do list.

Create real opportunities for employee involvement. Launch teams and committees to work on sustainability projects. Give official sanction to sustainability teams by providing them with the resources that they need to be successful and by allowing them to meet on work time. Asking groups to meet on their own time sends the message that this is not integral to real work. These efforts should also be given visibility and public acknowledgement for the accomplishments that they achieve.

Take symbolic actions. Identify symbolic management actions that will demonstrate leadership's commitment to the efforts. For example, when the president of the Oregon Museum of Science and Industry wanted to support the employee-driven effort to encourage commuting via alternative transportation, we suggested that she ride her bike to work and then, before cleaning up, make sure at least a dozen people saw her sweaty and still wearing her bike helmet.

EMPLOYEES DON'T SEE THE RELEVANCE OF SUSTAINABILITY TO THEIR INDIVIDUAL JOBS

Often we find that employees get excited about sustainability but are at a loss as to what it means that they should do differently on a day-to-day basis. It's important for organizations to make explicit the link between a sustainability initiative and each person's job. For example, an environmental agency had code enforcement officials who thought their job was strictly to interpret and enforce the existing regulations. We helped them to examine their duties in light of sustainability. They uncovered opportunities to offer consulting services in conjunction with their code reviews, making suggestions to customers about how they might meet (and exceed) the code by applying principles of sustainability in their projects. They still fulfilled their original obligations, but added a valuable and educative service to customers at the same time. This improved their relationship with those whom they regulated and made them feel better about their work.

Employees often know intuitively that what they are doing is not sustainable, but have trouble determining what to do differently. Below are a set of strategies that we have seen organizations employ to overcome this confusion.

Conduct an impact assessment at the work group or individual job level. Help employees to explicitly map out their inputs, outputs and key activities. Then assess these impacts against your sustainability framework. This will enable them to see where their impacts are and expose opportunities for change and improvement (see Chapter 4).

Do backcasting at the work group level. Help employees to break out of a day-to-day focus by thinking far into the future in the same way you do for your organization as a whole. Ask what their function would look like in 20 years if it were completely sustainable. What would they be doing and what would they not be doing? Working backwards from that distant vision, help them to see how tasks would evolve over time by asking what would they need to be doing in ten years in order to achieve that 20-year vision. And in order to implement the ten-year goals, what would they need to be doing in the next five years? Continue this backward chaining process until they identify the immediate tasks that will move them toward the vision of sustainability.

Share inspiring stories. Another useful strategy is to share stories from other parts of the organization, or even other organizations, that illustrate how people are applying sustainability to similar functions. Whenever possible, use near-peers, people who are similar in level and type of work. We love telling office workers, for example, about the law firm we discovered that is virtually paperless. When people see for themselves what people in similar positions or sectors are doing, they can assess their own practices in a new light. Even better, take people on site visits or bring in speakers so that employees can hear the stories directly from the people involved.

Employ a checklist or assessment tool. Some assessments translate the abstract notion of sustainability into terms, methods and actions for a particular industry or function. Two examples are the Leadership in Energy and Environmental Design (LEED) standard developed by the US Green Building Council and the Sustainability Competency and Opportunity Rating and Evaluation (SCORE) assessment developed by AXIS. Taking employees through instruments like these will help to translate the lofty principles of sustainability into day-to-day tasks. There are also certain sustainability frameworks that lay out principles for a specific industry. Examples include the Equator Principles for the financial industry, the *Talloires Declaration* for higher education and the Melbourne Principles for sustainable communities. You may be able to use these principles in the same manner.

IT TAKES EXTRA EFFORT TO DO THE RIGHT THING

Some employees care enough to go out of their way to behave sustainably; but for many, you have to make sustainability easy or automatic. This requires embedding sustainability within the organization's structures, policies and business systems. This is the ultimate form of integration: the point at which the sustainable option becomes the normal way of doing business. You want sustainability to be the default, not the exception.

Change the physical environment. Our physical environment has a big impact upon the way in which we behave. SERA Architects in Portland, Oregon, for example, removed all the waste bins under employees' desks and replaced them with paper recycling bins. Now, if employees really want to throw something away, they have to cross the office to find the single office rubbish bin. Many changes to the physical environment can be subtler. Consider setting the default on all your printers and copiers to double-sided printing so that people don't have to make the conscious choice. If you have automated purchasing systems, be sure the 'green' supplies come up first in the choice of options. When you are remodelling your office or planning a move, incorporate sustainable materials within your design and locate your office so that employees can take advantage of more sustainable transportation options.

Rewrite organizational policies. Policies determine behaviour as well. Rewrite your purchasing policies to reflect your commitment to sustainability. Include sustainability language in your vendor contracts and shift your 401K investments to socially responsible funds. Make sure that you are not inadvertently encouraging unsustainable behaviour with policies such as subsidizing parking or providing Styrofoam cups in your break rooms.

Adapt your management systems. Your performance management systems are probably the most powerful levers of behaviour change at your disposal. Adapt your systems for evaluating and rewarding employees to ensure that sustainability is truly integrated within their jobs. Fold sustainability criteria into hiring standards so that you are recruiting people who can understand and support your efforts. Promote people that take sustainability seriously or achieve sustainable results. And, above all, make sure that your performance metrics at the organizational, department and individual level are regularly reviewed and discussed.

CONCLUSION

Sustainability is too important to the survival of our planet and our economy to risk poor implementation. We can take advantage of the lessons learned by the pioneers in this field to ensure that sustainable practices take hold in our organizations and prevent the 'flavour of the month' syndrome. Sustainability, after all, isn't something extra people do; it is the new standard for the way in which things need to be done.

Appendix 2
Team Pre-launch Handout and Worksheet

TEAM PRE-LAUNCH: FIVE FOUNDATION CONCEPTS

Involvement engenders support. Research has long shown that people are far more likely to support something they were involved in creating, even if it's not in their own personal self-interest.

> *Moral: assign to the team those who have relevant perspectives, as well as people who must understand and support the change.*

Cost of inefficient meetings. It's well worth the time to plan the team charter carefully, as well as individual meetings, because one wasted hour can represent hundreds of dollars of staff time ... not to mention the frustration.

> *Moral: conduct a structured pre-launch and plan to spend as much time planning each meeting as facilitating.*

Group process is the key to leveraging the brains in the room. Some will monopolize the meeting if you don't have good methods for balancing participation, capturing ideas, coming to consensus and reiterating commitments. Well-managed teams can often make better decisions on complex issues than individuals.

> *Moral: use a skilled facilitator.*

Power is part of empowerment. Too often, managers ask teams to consider options and get back to them with recommendations. This sets up the frustration-inducing 'that's not what I meant' response to proposals. But rights bring an equal level of responsibility to make decisions in the best interest of the organization.

> *Moral: be clear about your boundaries so that you can give the team the power to decide, not recommend. And give the team responsibilities to implement, not just plan.*

Clear fences make strong teams. Some managers think that they will disempower the team if they are too specific about what they want and expect. Instead, the opposite is the case. Research shows that clear boundaries encourage creativity and risk-taking.

> *Moral: think long and hard about the boundary conditions for the team, representing all relevant stakeholder expectations and requirements. The team will know what they have the power to decide and what they can only recommend.*

PRELIMINARY TEAM CHARTER

WHY

Organization	Team members

WHAT

Description of the task:	
Questions to answer:	Measures of success:
Boundary conditions: What the team doesn't have the authority to do	

WHO

Representing	Individuals or process to get them

WHEN/WHERE

Step/timeframe				

HOW

Givens	Hopes

FACILITATION PLAN: INITIAL MEETING

This is a generic meeting agenda for the first team meeting.

Meeting purpose: Clarify the team charter, roles and operational guidelines to ensure the team's success.			
Date	Time	Location	Attendees and roles

Time	Outcome	Process and materials (who)	Results/decisions/to do's
	Welcome members and impress upon them the importance of their participation and the organization's gratitude.		
	Have members get to know one another and begin to develop trust.		
	Ensure that the purpose, expectations and boundaries are clear to all team members.		
	Identify concerns and needs that the team may have to be successful and decide on solutions.		
	Get volunteers for needed team roles.		
	Develop a schedule of meetings.		
	Develop team guidelines for operation.		
	Confirm to-do's and next steps.		

FACILITATION PLAN

This is a template for future meetings.

Meeting purpose:			
Date	Time	Location	Attendees

Time	Outcome	Process and materials (who)	Results/decisions/to do's

Index